Educator Wellbeing

Educator Wellbeing, written in response to the 2020 global pandemic, speaks to the long-ignored expectations that Educators live with, and the impact on their wellbeing that going above and beyond to serve their students has. This book is a relatable and practical read for teachers to build tools for life, bringing their wellbeing to the forefront. It provides a toolbox of preventative and responsive strategies to help Educators look after their wellbeing so they can continue with supporting their students.

Madhavi Nawana Parker provides a supportive and practical wellbeing framework that can be tailored to meet teachers' unique and personal needs, and supports theory with personal vignettes to bring to life topics such as:

- Areas for improved wellbeing in the current climate
- Giving yourself permission to prioritise wellbeing
- Wellbeing for Educators going forward

A timely response to an international event with far-reaching effects, *Educator Wellbeing* has never been more needed by practitioners, as a contemporary answer and basis for a new tradition of supportive practice.

Madhavi Nawana Parker is a behavioural consultant, working in schools and allied healthcare settings, specialising in building cultures of wellbeing, resilience, social-emotional intelligence and confidence. Madhavi is a keynote and public speaker, widely published author, counsellor in private practice and director of Positive Minds Australia.

"An exceptional resource to foster resilience and support the wellbeing of Educators. The concrete strategies and experiential exercises are underpinned by proven psychological principles and presented in a dynamic and engaging manner."

Chris Clements, *Psychologist and Teacher, Pulteney Grammar School, South Australia*

"Acknowledging and insightful into the responsibilities and rewards experienced by Educators, this engaging book can be read from cover to cover or casually flipped open to start where it suits you. Here's a book you will recommend to others and return to again and again."

Jen Bratovic, *Education Team Manager, Australia*

"An invaluable framework with a true understanding of Education, the joys of teaching and the pressures of schools. Relevant, practical and concise, full of opportunities to implement reflective practices, cultivate optimism and to reset. This incredible resource can be used for personal gain or as a leading dialogue with staff, to build a world-class culture of wellbeing."

Nicolle Stephanos, *Education Consultant, Australia*

"Beautifully written, hailing Educators and acknowledging the importance of preserving their wellbeing. Packed with strategies that foster strong and resilient emotional health, this is a valuable read for all Educational leaders and Educators."

Ali Thomson, *School Principal, South Australia*

Educator Wellbeing
Practical Solutions to Reset, Recharge and Recover

Madhavi Nawana Parker

LONDON AND NEW YORK

First edition published 2021
by Routledge
2 Park Square, Milton Park, Abingdon, Oxon, OX14 4RN

and by Routledge
52 Vanderbilt Avenue, New York, NY 10017

Routledge is an imprint of the Taylor & Francis Group, an informa business

© 2021 Madhavi Nawana Parker

The right of Madhavi Nawana Parker to be identified as author of this work has been asserted by her in accordance with sections 77 and 78 of the Copyright, Designs and Patents Act 1988.

All rights reserved. No part of this book may be reprinted or reproduced or utilised in any form or by any electronic, mechanical, or other means, now known or hereafter invented, including photocopying and recording, or in any information storage or retrieval system, without permission in writing from the publishers.

Trademark notice: Product or corporate names may be trademarks or registered trademarks, and are used only for identification and explanation without intent to infringe.

British Library Cataloguing-in-Publication Data
A catalogue record for this book is available from the British Library

Library of Congress Cataloging-in-Publication Data
A catalog record for this book has been requested

ISBN: 978-0-367-61553-6 (hbk)
ISBN: 978-0-367-61555-0 (pbk)
ISBN: 978-1-003-10548-0 (ebk)

Typeset in Bembo
by Apex CoVantage, LLC

This book is dedicated to you, the Educator.
May you always know just how much you matter.

Contents

Acknowledgements		viii
Foreword by Shawn Hutchinson		xiii
	Introduction	1
1	What the 2020 Global Pandemic highlighted about Educator wellbeing	4
2	Resetting for healthy wellbeing	14
3	Recharging your wellbeing battery	35
4	A license to rest and recover	49
5	Where to from here? Making wellbeing comebacks, not wellbeing 'go backs'	65
6	Stories of courage, hope and endurance: wellbeing during crisis and challenge	86
7	Where to from here?	94
	Index	96

Acknowledgements

Nothing happens in isolation. I'm grateful for the love, guidance and support I've had my whole life on both a personal and professional level.

Professional acknowledgements

Thank you Alison Foyle, Senior Publisher, Routledge, London, for your heartfelt enthusiasm, steady guidance and ongoing encouragement. This book emerged from a conversation between us about Educator Wellbeing during the Global Pandemic. Your confidence in me as an author and professional allowed me to write with such ease and to come out the other end energised instead of exhausted. I look forward to being in the same country again so we can enjoy a conversation and meal together. I admire and appreciate you as a person and also as an advisor.

Thank you to Routledge and Taylor & Francis, UK and Australia, for enthusiastically taking on the mammoth task of producing my book from my manuscript to print in record time during a time our workplaces were adjusting and adapting to many unexpected changes. Special thanks to Leah Burton, Alex Butterworth and James Robbins, Routledge, for your ongoing professionalism and excellence.

Thank you to the kind, hardworking and talented Lauren Eldridge Murray for yet another beautiful book cover. You wholeheartedly took my brief into your hands, understanding the value of Educators, considering the content seamlessly and days later producing a front cover I'm hugely grateful for. You did all of this during a pandemic with three young children and made every interaction a joy. You are a beautiful person, an exceptional artist and someone I am very grateful to have in my life.

Thank you to my friend, confidante and very first professional mentor, Amanda Harris, psychologist. You have been there from the very beginning of my career. Listening, cheering me on and sharing my love and curiosity for this work. We get as excited to see each other today as we did 20 years ago. You are truly one of my greatest blessings. Thank you Nicolle Stephanos for always being 'McFunny,' starting out as my student, then my colleague, sounding board and wise leader in Education. Growing together as professionals from the start of our careers at Autism SA has been a uniquely joyful and enriching experience. Thank you to the legendary Educators I work with every day in schools. You carry out your work with a level of care, intelligence and professionalism I admire and respect. I'm lucky to know and learn from all of you. While I can't mention everyone personally, because the list would be too long, a special mention to everyone at two of my weekly consulting schools, Pulteney Grammar School and Scotch College. Thank you for being so brilliant to work with and for welcoming and supporting mine and Nikki Wadewitz's work with your students.

Thank you to the Wellbeing champions in schools, who do everything possible to support the mental health and wellbeing of young people. I hope you will read this book and put the heart and soul you dedicate to your students back to yourself. A very special mention to Danielle Verrilli, Natalie Carling, Chris Catt, Carmen Fiedler and Kasey Thorne, all stellar human beings, who so promptly read and reviewed my book proposal, despite your incredibly full workloads. I love knowing all of you as people and as professionals. I appreciate your ongoing support of both my writing and my work. What you do each day in schools is above and beyond anything I could and I hold you all in the highest esteem.

Thank you Shawn Hutchinson, Head of School, AGC School Jakarta, Indonesia, Member of Inspired Education, for generously offering your time to write the Foreword and make a comment for Chapter One. Your authentic leadership, integrity and excellence impacts greatly on the global teaching community. What a privilege to have your words on these pages. Thank you to the fabulous Pulteney Grammar School Psychologist, Chris Clements, for embracing and reading my manuscript – and kindly writing a comment for my back cover. Thank you Ali Thomson, School Principal, for being so enthusiastic after reading the manuscript and finding time to write a book endorsement, despite your heavy work load. Thank you Jen Bratovic, Education Team Manager, for reading the manuscript, wishing it well with such a generous heart and for the privilege of having your words on the back cover. Thank you Nicolle Stephanos for connecting me to Ali and Jen and for reading and valuing the manuscript so much. I admire the incredible work all of you do each day that paves the way for the future of Education.

Thank you Dr Gill Hicks, Nicholas Lee, Melissa Little and Derrick McManus for welcoming an interview with me for Chapter Six, where you inspire others through your stories, courage, insight, experience and character. It was a joy to collaborate and a privilege to have you share your heart with me. You're such exemplary human beings, whose authenticity, integrity, honesty and warmth were infectious. I am hugely grateful to include you in my book so others can grow from your knowledge and experience. I wish all of you the very best, always.

Thank you to the gorgeous Educators Lucy Radford, Jo Porter, Emma McKenzie, Skye Forde, Shari and others who shared their thoughts with me for Chapter One. I know how busy you all are, yet my call to support others by sharing your stories grabbed your attention and you acted on it. Your compassion for your colleagues and best wishes for your field allowed you to find the time to do this (despite my asking right in the middle of a mammoth learning curve in Education). Your honesty and clarity in your comments will no doubt bring comfort and inspiration to others. Your students are fortunate to have your ongoing leadership and compassion.

Thank you to all the young people, parents and professionals I work with every day who make it easy for me to do my best for you. I have known many of you for years and my work with you is a matter of the heart, not just the mind. Thank you for the privilege of allowing me to help you navigate your ups, downs, twists and turns. It is always a pleasure to come to work and see you.

Thank you to the Positive Minds Australia team; I love knowing and working with all of you. I'm forever grateful for the compassion and professionalism you bring to work each day. My work is so much stronger because of the wisdom, creativity and intelligence you add to our organisation.

Thank you Vashti Starling, my beautiful personal assistant, for taking on everything I'm rubbish at and making it look so easy. Thank you for compiling consent forms, endorsements and Educator comments for this book under a tight deadline and also for being such a joy to work with. Thank you Nikki Wadewitz for bringing 100 percent dedication to work with you every day. I couldn't have made my manuscript deadline without your Anzac biscuits and the hilarious notes and text messages either. Thank you James Parker, my sounding board and 'Chief Advisor,' for continually supporting and encouraging my personal and professional growth. Thank you Nick Bennett for all the extra care you take every day to make life that bit better for your students. I admire your gentle patience and excellence whenever I get to work with you. Thank you Katie O'Reilly for making every work conversation a comedy that always ends up in something brilliant. I'm so grateful for your creativity, commitment, compassion and friendship. Thank you Kym Siddons, Leah Vermeeran, Anita McCurdie and Emma McKenzie for the enthusiasm, dedication and time you've contributed to our team. I am so grateful for each of you.

Thank you Autism SA, my first job out of University in the late 1990s, where I first understood the importance of social emotional health and wellbeing and made many lifelong friends including Kate Rayner, Melanie Dolphin and Amanda Harris. Thank you to the hard working, funny and wise Mark Le Messurier, my friend and co-author of the 'What's the Buzz?' books and resources. It is such a privilege to write with and know you. Thank you to my beautiful colleagues and friends Rose Price, John Hall, Bill Hansberry, Kay Bosworth, Karen Hodson and Benita Ranzon from Fullarton House who I learnt so much from and loved sharing a private practice with.

Thank you to all the other professionals I know and work with who contribute to my professional growth every day. I am grateful to know and learn from all of you.

Personal thanks

Thank you to my kind, compassionate and wise parents, Srinath Nawana and Mallika Nawana, for bringing me into this world and honouring their role with love, care and guidance. I couldn't have asked for a better start to life. I will always honour the lessons you taught me growing up. Thank you to my brother and sister, Namal Nawana and Srimal Nawana, my first friends before the big wide world, and to their children, my precious nieces and nephews Dylan, Elea, Tylanni and Nael, who bring me so much joy. Thank you to my extended family in Sri Lanka and around the world.

Thank you to the loves of my life, my husband, James, and our children, Soraya, Toby and Zach. I love you guys way beyond the moon (and zoo) and back. No matter how much I talk, there will never be enough words to express how I feel about you. Instead, you have to put up with me greeting you like it's been three decades since I last saw you, every single day. You make everything in my life possible. I love nothing more than your gentle and loving company. You are my greatest blessings. I am so proud of all of you.

Thank you to my beautiful friends. I know I'm going to miss someone on this list but I'm feeling brave to name some of you. If you think you should have been on the list, please tell me and know I will feel bad for the rest of my life. Sally Bolton, may we always talk over each other, yet never miss a beat. I don't know how I got so lucky to have you in my life. We've experienced teenage-hood, adulthood, weddings, parenthood, sickness and health and I will never take what we've shared for granted over the last 30 something years. I love how you see the best in everyone and everything. Here's to beautiful flowers and coffee by us. Tania Campbell, who feels everything deeply with one of the most loving hearts I've had the privilege of knowing, I am forever grateful for our lifelong friendship. We laugh, we cry, we laugh again. When I walk past your family home, it always makes me smile as I think of you and the fun we shared growing up together. Ange O'Halloran, my first friend with a car who told me going out for coffee after school was a thing (as was shopping for clothes on King William Road) to now, where pyjamas and coffee via Zoom on a Friday night hits the right spot. I love that we always find a way to laugh together, no matter what is going on in our lives. To my other Unley High School friends – too many to mention, I love that we're still friends. I hope we can have our reunion at the end of 2020 as planned by our 'Rising Sun' committee. Oh my goodness, how good were those chips?

Thank you, Leanne Schmidt, for never saying a word against that holograph top I wore in my 20s (yikes), for growing your own diamond, the hilarious letters we exchanged through University and for always being there. Thank you Rebecca (Bec) Barr for being a steady and loyal friend, introducing me to avocadoes on toast when we were 19 and for looking so grateful when I made your wedding cake, despite it ending up on a major lean. Thank you Kari Bienart and Steve Warwyck for all the years of love and friendship we shared from Adelaide University to Cha-Chi's to Rundle Street and beyond. Nicolle Stephanos, never forgetting to hang up on 19 minutes in our 20s to being a consistent, lifelong friend who goes above and beyond not only with our friendship but in every aspect of your life. I love and appreciate you. Amanda Harris, may we always clap with joy every time we see each other. I love you so much. To my beautiful GOPS, STJK and GIHS school mum friends – what a gift you all are to me. Thank you for always being a joy to see on school run (I'm not naming names – it's far too dangerous). To the beautiful 'girls in the neighbourhood,' who I am completely and utterly blessed to share friendship, motherhood chats, laughter and 'champagnola' with: Katie O'Reilly, Audrey Woodrow, Vashti Tyrell, Rebecca Payne, Sascha Smith, Vanessa Wigg, Margot Solomon, Sally Venus, Kate Bolton, Tania Sulan and Meaghan Thomas. I love our walks, talks, spontaneous pop ins and enthusiastic waves while driving past each other. I love each and every one of you way more than coffee, chocolate and miniature food.

Thank you to my gym coach, Richard Mills, for your genuine commitment to keeping me fit; Peter Lindschau for politely noticing and redirecting me when I'm about to injure myself; and my gym mates for sharing the aches and pains, banter and laughter, long before the sun rises. To our beloved Jo Shanahan, who tragically lost her life way before her time while I was writing this book: May your gentle words, 'do your best, be kind and the rest will take care of itself,' continue to ripple far and wide. Rest in peace beautiful Jo. Your life mattered, you didn't waste a second and the world will never be the same again without you.

To anyone I've left off here and should have mentioned, I'm so very terribly sorry. I thank you from the bottom of my heart.

With love always,
Madhavi

Foreword

Like the 2020 Global Pandemic, Madhavi Nawana Parker's latest book provides us with an opportunity to learn and gain from our experiences, so we can consciously and deliberately move forward in ways that improve our lives. It provides a strong reminder that as Educators, we must not limit our support to the wellbeing of our students, their parents and carers. We must freely show ourselves the same compassion we show our students, turning our attention inwards and investing in our own wellbeing too. Educators work tirelessly and selflessly to teach students each day. This should not come at a cost to their Wellbeing.

My hope for Education and Educators around the world is that Wellbeing becomes a priority. I hope that books like this will lead to measurable improvements in teacher mental health, better work-life balance, and that the solutions offered here become part of the daily routines at preschools, primary and secondary schools, tertiary and vocational education institutions.

Madhavi Nawana Parker's book provides a practical and easy-to-read approach to develop essential tools to avoid burnout and prioritise self-care. If we want to see mentally healthy young people attending schools and institutions of further learning, then we must do all that we can to support our Educators and ensure that their health and wellbeing becomes the number one priority.

Shawn Hutchinson

Head of School, AGC School Jakarta, Indonesia,
Member of Inspired Education

Introduction

When the Global Pandemic of 2020 hit, the world turned upside down at a speed and intensity no one was prepared for. It wasn't the first occasion humanity faced an unexpected crisis and severe discomfort. Adversity has lived abundantly throughout history, since the beginning of time. The world was unified in its shared experience of grief, fear, uncertainty and change. Citizens were thrown towards quick decisions, problem solving, keeping calm yet vigilant and drawing upon courage and resilience they never knew possible. Many went in unprepared, already struggling and now pushed to their limits.

Educators' focus and dedication calls upon much more than teaching the academic curriculum. As part and parcel of the nature of their work, they often become mentors, counsellors, confidants, emotional coaches and in some cases 'surrogate carers' to their students. Educating young people is both gratifying and emotionally taxing. Educators are clever, stoic and remarkable beings whose wellbeing belongs at the forefront of any school.

Educator wellbeing has always been an uncertainty in the global school community. The 2020 Pandemic highlighted more than ever before just how much is expected from Educators and how hard Educators are willing to work and adapt to serve their students. The missing piece remains, as it has for far too long. What about Educator wellbeing? Who helps Educators through a crisis; and what, in fact, is the best way to help?

Educator Wellbeing: practical solutions to reset, recharge and recover provides a breath of fresh air. It is an accessible, relatable and practical read for Educators across the globe to build relatable tools for life that bring personal wellbeing to the forefront, without compromising existing standards of excellence in service delivery. It's the lifeline they've been waiting for. A solid framework of preventative, proactive and responsive strategies to help Educators engage in selfcare so they can continue the work they were born to do – the work only they know how to do so well. Educator wellbeing matters. We need our Educators to be okay.

What is wellbeing?

Your best thinking, mood and behaviour come when self-care and wellbeing are prioritised. Wellbeing is the foundation for better emotional health and resilience. Wellbeing is 'a state of being comfortable, healthy, or happy' (*Oxford Dictionary*, 2018). Wellbeing lies at the heart of a connected, fulfilled and joyful experience of life.

Educators already invest a lot of their time to the unofficial work of supporting student wellbeing, so the topic is not new to them. A career of service, commitment, dedication and, quite often, sacrifice can mean that personal wellbeing has taken a back seat for Educators for far too long. This book puts your wellbeing in the front seat, something many of you may not have experienced until now.

Mental health and wellbeing are nourished by self-compassion and self-care as well as involvement in character strength and personality-related endeavours. Creating a culture of wellbeing in every school, not only for students but also for Educators, provides a license to look after yourself the moment you enter your workplace. Student wellbeing will also improve when Educator Wellbeing becomes a priority. Emotions are contagious; we get them from others and give them to others. Educators absorb the emotional brunt of what their students express and carry this on their shoulders. Without daily recovery, they may in turn pass it back on to their students.

Wellbeing is the by-product of many things working together. Wellbeing is not an isolated skill like teaching someone how to read or ride a bike. There are multiple factors involved in developing and maintaining your wellbeing. Long-term resilience and wellbeing is primarily connected to strong healthy connections with significant others (Werner and Smith 2001).

It cannot be forced or rushed. Trying too hard to learn these skills and placing pressure on yourself to do so can be counter-productive. Developing wellbeing is a process; a combined result of many experiences across the lifetime, skills developed along the way and influenced further by individual personalities, temperaments, genetic predispositions and environmental influences (Hall and Pearson, 2001). Each Educator is unique and develops in their own way, in their own time, and each small step is a step closer to improved wellbeing.

Before you begin

This book is designed to make Educators' lives easier. It provides a simple, supportive and practical wellbeing framework that can be tailored to meet your unique and personal needs. You might read it cover to cover or take each tool one step at a time, giving yourself as much time as you need to learn and practice the skill and continue on to the next skill when you're ready. There may be some things you might need to unlearn and leave behind, because wellbeing is also about what you *don't* do. Again, this will happen at your own pace.

However you plan to go about it, make an agreement with yourself to do this at your own pace, without harshly judging your progress. For many of you, this may be the first time you have prioritised yourself. It might even be the first book you've read that is for your benefit and not your students. If you're feeling guilty about investing this time into your wellbeing then perhaps this will help. Our emotional state has a ripple effect onto everyone we know and interact with. Your healthy wellbeing will support your student's healthy wellbeing. You matter. When you surrender to letting yourself matter, you are modelling an important skill to them. So, there you go, you are about to create change that's not only good for you, but good for all.

Sustainable change

As you delve into the pages ahead, remember that not all healthy wellbeing tools are the right tools for you and where you're at right now. Try to avoid getting caught up in new strategies that aren't for you. You will seek and need different methods of wellbeing at different stages of your life. For change to be sustainable, choose what's possible and sensible to you that you can maintain long term.

The following questions will help provide you with a frame of reference about where your wellbeing is right now and where you'd like it to be when you've finished with this book. Try to take a moment and answer them before you get stuck in the book.

Wellbeing questions

> Which aspects of your wellbeing are strong and healthy right now? In other words, where in your physical and emotional health are you feeling well, balanced and nurtured?
> What are you already doing that improves your wellbeing?
> What are you doing that is not helpful to your wellbeing?
> What have you thought about doing for your wellbeing that you haven't got around to yet?
> If you had to rate your wellbeing out of ten (ten being perfect, five being okay and zero being terrible) what number would you choose? What number do you think is reasonable for you to be at given your personal circumstances?

It's time to bring your wellbeing to the forefront. The future of Education needs you to not only survive but to thrive.

Are you ready, Educators?

Let's begin . . .

References

Hall, D. and Pearson, J. (2001). Critical Abilities Related to the Development of Resilience. Interaction. Canadian Childcare Federation, Ottawa.

Werner, E. and Smith, S. (2001). *Journeys from Childhood to Midlife: Risk Resilience and Recovery*. Ithaca, NY: Cornell University Press.

1 What the 2020 Global Pandemic highlighted about Educator wellbeing

Some of you may be reading this book long after the pandemic. Others will have it in your hands while you're still navigating your way through it or dealing with the aftermath of having been through it. Whether you're in it or way past it, no Educator will ever forget its impact. This chapter highlights the challenges many of you experienced and overcame.

Educator wellbeing has been a long-standing and significant challenge in global school communities. Working in Education is way more than a job. It's a powerful legacy involving countless after hours planning without pay, early starts and late finishes, sleepless nights worrying about students, ongoing professional development and much more.

Covid-19 placed a global spotlight on a gap in Educators having tools to not only cope with the demands of their emotionally taxing work, but to respond to additional pressure during a crisis. With little or no warning, Educators were plunged into a rapid spin cycle of adapting and delivering high-quality education in amongst chaos and unpredictability. In a job already requiring so much more than teaching a curriculum, Educators were now responsible for keeping their students calm, helping parents learn how to assist with online learning and all the while going through the same shock and uncertainty everyone else did, as a pandemic swept the world over.

This chapter is an opportunity for Educators to begin their wellbeing path by reviewing what they went through and how far they've come. May it always be a reminder of what Educators resiliently and heroically rose up to and achieved in such a short amount of time. May it show newcomers to the field of Education, who may have joined the profession after the Global Pandemic, that this is the powerful, limitless capability of an Educator.

May it be a reminder that if anything like this ever happens again, Educators need to be prepared and supported, so they don't do all of this at the sacrifice of their wellbeing.

Why did the Global Pandemic feel like going to war?

It didn't take long to feel the ferocity of the virus. No one felt, or was, immune. Negative stories devastated the newsreel and the world went in to battle to 'flatten the curve.' A fight was on between a powerful, highly contagious killer and humanity. It was travelling fast, giving no secrets away, like a highly trained assassin. With no vaccine and high infection rates, the world had gone to war against something they felt completely powerless against.

Life changed.

Educators' usual methods of stress management (time with friends, sports, hobbies, going to the gym, going to restaurants and cafes) were shut down abruptly. Under these uniquely challenging circumstances, maintaining healthy wellbeing was, naturally, extremely difficult.

The loss of control and sense of constant defeat was interrupted with occasional glimpses of a flattening curve and feeling like things were looking up . . . soon followed by another peak and more tragic news. No one knew for sure what was going on and messages about how to respond were inconsistent and chaotic. Meanwhile, Educators continued on with the job of teaching in person for longer than most felt comfortable, followed by teaching online sooner than most felt prepared for.

Not having a sense of control or autonomy can lead to feelings of despair and anxiety. Focusing on what you can control is crucial during periods of shock, change and grief. Few people are aware of this small yet powerful wellbeing tool. By regaining a sense of control over variables in your power (like how much news you read and watch, your social media engagement, self-care rituals, engaging in things that bring you a sense of confidence and accomplishment, gratitude and presence) you're able to redirect your thinking and actions when things become too much. Educators, along with other essential services, didn't have the luxury of time to develop this knowledge or learn these skills. They had to keep going. A sense of control or autonomy was a far cry from their reality.

While the challenges of every day teaching pale in comparison to what Educators went through during the Global Pandemic, they are still very challenging. Whether it's managing a heavy workload, facing a difficult class dynamic, not feeling there's enough time to pause and catch your breath or struggling to find the sweet spot for teaching a disengaged student, your job as an Educator has inevitable daily challenges.

Now you've achieved something as colossal as keeping yourself and your students safe in what felt like a battlefield, it's time to invest in recovery and looking forward towards resetting and recharging your healthy wellbeing.

All the 'what ifs'

Educators, while not directly treating the ill, were in a different kind of 'frontline' to healthcare workers. They worked hands on until schools closed, in classrooms full of young people with no guaranteed health clearance. It didn't take long for Educators' minds to be swamped by all the 'what ifs.'

What if you unknowingly contracted the virus somewhere and then gave it to your students, who would then spread it far and wide? What if you unknowingly contracted the virus at school and passed it on to your family? What if you were asymptomatic and have been a carrier for some time?

All the 'what ifs' made Educators feel understandably anxious, unable to think clearly and confidently; especially considering Educators, like other essential workers, didn't have the luxury of choosing whether or not they came into work.

Impact beyond the classroom

Many Educators felt frustrated during the pandemic, with the very real struggle of continuing as an Educator and supporting their students while also experiencing their own personal challenges like everyone else. Educators also experienced fear of job loss, worry about contagion, stress about bringing the virus home to their families; they were helping their own children adapt to online learning, having small businesses fold, partners losing their jobs and so on. They were in a rapidly changing environment, adapting and reinventing themselves, being exposed to large groups of young people where social distancing was impossible (before school shut down completely) with the background noise of their own lives.

When Educators got home from work, they couldn't greet their families in the usual way and launched into a crucial hygiene ritual – just in case they had been exposed that day. Cleaning and hygiene fatigue didn't take long to arrive. It's no wonder they reported such feelings of overwhelming stress. Covid-19 was affecting every aspect of their life and wellbeing. There was no break from staring the pandemic right in the eye.

The emotional rollercoaster

When you go through a more than usual life challenge or crisis, it's only natural your emotions will be less predictable. You can feel on top of everything one moment and completely lost the next. Progressing through change and the associated feelings doesn't happen in a straight line. At first, Educators put their super hero capes on, as they had done many times before, and rose to the challenge, resiliently collaborating to make things work for their students. Many felt they could handle it. That was until the immediate and long-term social, emotional, economic and health impacts of the crisis became abundantly clear – right alongside the overwhelming reality that a hopeful heart and solid work ethic was not enough to sustain Educators through the pressure and expectation placed upon them. This was much bigger than just figuring out how to teach online.

Emotional rollercoasters are a tough ride and Educators spent most of the Global Pandemic on one. Some are still trying to get off. It's time to return the favour by allowing Educators to put themselves first this time and develop the tools to build a solid wellbeing foundation that will sustain them now and well into the future.

Pretending to be okay when you're not okay

Amongst all the upheaval and uncertainty of the Global Pandemic, Educators had the additional responsibility of maintaining calm and confidence to support their students' wellbeing first and foremost. There was an unspoken rule it seemed to be to not complain, to take it all in stride, adapt fast and appear to be on top of things. Meanwhile, the learning curve was massive.

In the early days in particular, many Educators felt the pressure to keep it all together for the sake of the children, while politely tucking their own personal feelings away from public view.

While some days were better than others, the demands of adjusting to new routines, teaching young people about vigilant hygiene and social distancing, transferring to online learning with some students already at home and others still at school, was demanding to say the least. When schools closed down, Educators were teaching online, trying to support their students while also taking care of their own families. Those Educators who were parents were managing this while supporting their own childrens' distance learning, too.

Job uncertainty for relief teachers and school support officers became higher, adding the fear of job loss. Educators were watching other workplaces close their doors and ask staff to stay home and socially isolate. Some teachers and school support officers reported feelings of wanting to leave the profession during the peak of their anxiety about contracting Covid-19. Many feared admitting that they were struggling or experiencing anxiety and sadness. All these mixed feelings around a profession they genuinely loved and cared about was unravelling their sense of wellbeing.

Being able to express your feelings without fear of judgement is crucial for your wellbeing. When you find yourself unable to talk openly for whatever reason, remember there are other avenues you can turn towards.

To start thinking about this, take a moment to write the names of five people (or professionals/online services) where you can seek non-judgemental support and advice.

There may be a long way to go where help seeking is seen not only as natural, but necessary. Do everything you can to find courage to seek help, from that first moment you feel like you're struggling but, for whatever reason, can't talk openly about it yet.

Post traumatic amnesia

First of all, I'm not sure there is officially such a thing as 'post traumatic amnesia,' but the phrase seemed fitting for what I'm about to write here. I've been around for a while and one thing I've noticed is when a crisis occurs, after the initial shock, people have a natural tendency to grow accustomed to the situation. They soon forget what was learned and return to 'normal,' like nothing even happened. At the time of crisis, we collectively pause and take it all in. We meaningfully examine what's happened and do what we can to contribute to improving the situation. We even plan how we are going to learn, grow and come out stronger than ever. After a while, it's like we get amnesia. It's like nothing happened. There is rarely time to process everything and reset.

Covid-19 was much more than a health crisis. It was a global economic, emotional and psychological breakdown of everything we once knew. Coming out of social isolation is not going to miraculously heal the pain of social isolation, especially for those who lost loved ones during lockdown and couldn't collectively grieve. A vaccine isn't going to erase the anxiety that emerged when we were all drowning in the fear of contagion and seeing people lose their lives all around the world. Economic resurgence isn't going to repair the damage of what job loss and insecurity felt like and returning to school isn't going to subtract from the upheaval and exhaustion of distance learning.

Life can't just go back. Not without working through the consequences of what we experienced, anyway. This doesn't mean we have to spend months and years reflecting on it. There simply need to be opportunities to reset, recharge and recover. To talk about feelings and to adapt yet again to this new phase. Once there has been time for that – a process for that – the mind can let go and flourish yet again.

What people didn't know

To end this chapter, I ask you to take a moment to remember what you went through that you didn't talk about. Acknowledge it and feel proud you overcame such a lonely, tiring and frightening time. Next time you look back on what you went through, try moving beyond the upset feelings and welcome, instead, feelings of pride and accomplishment.

It's time to look ahead and put you first, so you can have the healthiest wellbeing of your life – and keep it that way. The world needs you to be okay. Educators are the custodians of much more than teaching a curriculum, they influence and tighten the global social thread.

In Educator's words . . .

The following showcases what a handful of teachers, principals, school support officers, school psychologists and other Educators had to say about the impact the Global Pandemic had on them. Most have their names published and others requested that their names be withheld. There were also many Educators whose heartfelt and useful comments could not be included without surpassing my word limit. I'm so grateful for their time as well.

Here, they share their heart with us: what kept them going and what they love about the work they do each day, to benefit the growth of the next generation.

From Shawn Hutchinson, Head of School, ACG School Jakarta, Indonesia (Member of Inspired Education)

On 2 March 2020, ACG School Jakarta was thrust into virtual schooling as we made the decision to temporarily close our campus in response to Covid-19 measures. One of our teachers had tested positive to the virus and was one of the first known cases in Indonesia. We spent weeks prior observing and learning from our colleagues in China and Vietnam, but nothing could prepare us fully for the journey we have undertaken. We are now in our fourteenth week of virtual schooling and will sadly end this academic year with an online Graduation, Prizegiving and End of Year Assembly. As we have a transient international school community made up of 70 % expatriate students and families, we will have to say goodbye to teachers, students and parents who are relocating from Indonesia to their next international posts. Our school re-opening contingency plans for an August start focuses on three possible scenarios including face-to-face instruction, a hybrid model of face-to-face and online learning, or the continuation of full virtual schooling. Although the future is very uncertain at this time, we remain optimistic about the future of education and move forward with new learning and how we adapt to virtual and hybrid models and take a blended approach back to the future.

Within 24 hours, we moved from closing our campus to delivering a full virtual school experience to students from Kindergarten to Year 13. We released virtual school guidelines to staff, students and parents and although we hoped for a brief quarantine and isolation period, we braced ourselves for the long haul. As we developed our operational contingency documents to be released to faculty and staff members through the crisis, we remained committed to ensuring the safety and wellbeing of our community. This commitment to safety and wellbeing has always been at the heart of our work as a learning community, but never before has 'wellbeing' driven decision-making like it has during this Global Pandemic.

Most of us are in privileged positions and certainly in the context of international education, we are very fortunate to live and work in such wonderful schools around the globe. Alongside our privilege and good fortune, we observe others less fortunate and observe poverty, limited access to health care and unbelievable injustices. We also often actively support the amazing work of global and local agencies, charities and support networks. However, during this Global Pandemic, the health, safety and wellbeing of Educators has once again become a hot topic and discussion point for members of our society. Why does it take a global pandemic for the education sector to acknowledge and address the importance of Educator wellbeing? The answer to that question may be obvious. We've often prioritised academic excellence, staffing efficiencies, facility developments, but place Educator wellbeing somewhere between the middle to the bottom of our priorities.

As we moved into delivering virtual schooling, we very quickly realized that our teachers, teacher assistants and support personnel were working 12–15 hours a day planning, delivering and reflecting upon synchronous and asynchronous lessons and assessments. Our teachers would respond to student, parent and colleague emails, make video conference calls to parents and students to check on the wellbeing of their students and follow up on attendance, provide detailed feedback to students, record videos and plan for the next day's lessons. So, what did we do to support Educator wellbeing? Well, one of the most important steps we took was to deliberately and regularly connect faculty members. Establishing an ongoing buddy system, having the academic leadership team make contact with staff members daily, actively promote and provide online counselling for faculty (both in-house and through outside agencies), support staff with existing health conditions to return to their home countries, support single teachers to return to their home countries, provide staff with digital data plans as they taught from home, celebrated birthdays with Zoom parties, coordinated social media contributions, and took every opportunity to connect with our community. We set up virtual school digital channels where teachers could share best practice, collaborate and access resources to support each other as they moved from a regular classroom experience to an online learning environment. We encouraged faculty members to share videos about what they were doing for fun, enjoyment and relaxation and this saw our teachers share yoga, cooking and even roller blading demonstrations.

***

From Skye Forde, primary school teacher, Australia

When the Global Pandemic hit, it was surreal. Life was changing at an alarming rate. My once routine and predictable classroom felt like it had been caught in a whirlwind. It was hard to go on like normal when outside our classroom walls it was changing. I felt like I couldn't keep up with it, there was so much information. It was scary and we could all feel the anxiety hanging in the air.

Pure adrenaline was what kept me going – and knowing that I was the teacher. I was the one who needed to reassure parents. I needed to answer my student's questions, I had to try my very best to be the calm in the storm. The expectation to lead, to have the answers and to be invincible was the only option. We had four days to totally transfer our whole way of teaching into an online classroom experience. At the same time, our own families and lives were being turned upside down.

An unexpected gift was for a brief moment we saw what was most important for our students. Despite the pressure when restrictions relaxed to return to teaching like Covid never happened, I resisted the push to focus on test scores rather than social skills. I am prioritising teaching emotional intelligence and the benefits to my students are showing already. I have learnt to slow down with my students, laugh with them, dance with them, teach them the joys of jigsaws and hopscotch, without success criteria or learning intentions. From this experience I will take away the importance of connection. When life looked scary and everything we knew as normal went out the window, it was all we had. It was all we wanted. It was all we needed. Yet so many students don't have it with anyone. I see more clearly now what a teacher needs to do.

***

From Lucy Radford, year 2 classroom teacher, South Australia

I was immediately surrounded by leadership and a community that provided guidance and information that was relevant and specific to our setting. It was so important to maintain normality and continuity for students. I helped achieve this by honestly answering any questions they had, supporting parents and families with their concerns, while providing a safe environment for the children to play, interact and learn.

The students and staff I work with kept me going. We implemented an online learning programme within a week, something we had been trialling (in terms of assessment for data collection) to implement for years. I learnt so much in that week and the weeks following about how online learning can enhance teaching and learning. It also allowed me to teach from home as I am pregnant. My school supported me to work from home for as long as was necessary. This made me feel a valued member of the school and teaching community.

An unexpected gift was that a student in my class who has selective mutism and previously did not speak in the classroom was verbally engaging with the online content, freely voicing his ideas and opinions through the online learning platform. I was so moved to hear his voice and to hear his knowledge and understanding, it was such a positive outcome. We are currently working on strategies to build confidence to translate his online learning skills into the classroom.

***

From Shari, school support officer, Australia

When the pandemic hit, school routines changed quickly and things got so much busier. This made the children I worked with more anxious than usual. We scrambled to get resources together to help them and worried about vulnerable students. As a school support officer, working 1:1 with students with disabilities didn't allow for social distancing, so that was stressful. The kids kept me going. That's who we're here for after all. An unexpected gift was seeing the strengthening of relationships amongst the students as the attendance numbers dwindled; some unexpected friendships evolved too.

***

From a school psychologist, Melbourne, Australia

I'm exhausted. I've been doing this job and loving it for over 23 years. Switching to online video counselling completely threw me. I struggle with technology as it is, but having to communicate through a screen is really hard for me. It just doesn't come naturally and I feel like I'm 'acting' all the time. I feel like I have to make myself more interesting to make up for not being in the same room. I guess I'm just 'old school.' I get so much from being in the same room as my students. Online counselling doesn't flow easily for me and even though the children are really grateful to stay connected and continue to make progress, it really makes me doubt myself because I see other psychologists and counsellors doing really well with the technology. Many of them say they love it. I want to be in a room again with my students, to sense their feelings and respond accordingly. I miss them so much.

***

From Jo Porter, assistant principal, South Australia, 30+ years in Education

Being in a leadership position meant we were stuck between following Government guidelines which required we continued working face to face, while ensuring staff felt heard, valued and supported. The school holidays arriving at the peak of the pandemic was timely and being in isolation meant it was one of the best holiday breaks I've ever had! It was a real opportunity to recharge, get back to basics and enjoy the simple things in life.

I have felt incredibly lucky throughout these strange times. My job was secure and I got to come to work and be around wonderful people every day. Many of my colleagues are also dear friends and I felt lucky to have still had the opportunity to 'socialise' and feel 'normal.' Kids have a way of keeping you grounded too. We experienced enormous appreciation and gratitude from our parent community, which meant a lot to me.

My favourite aspect of Education, without a doubt, is the relationships – with students, parents, staff – that's what it's all about for me. Getting to know families, watching children grow and knowing that you have had a positive impact along the way is the best reward you could hope for. I have tried a few different jobs over the years and keep coming back to Education because nothing else has ever felt meaningful enough.

***

From a school support officer, South Australia

I felt really scared when I was going to work at school and most of my friends and family were socially isolating. It was impossible to keep my distance from students. I'm an SSO and most of my students are used to sitting close and needing my help to be calm and do their work. I couldn't turn them away, but I was also afraid. Most of them are really touchy feely and I felt guilty for flinching when they touched my things and sat close. I think that time was the most stressed I have ever been in my whole life. We were lucky in South Australia and things were contained really quickly. I feel really bad for schools around the world who have to keep this going for months. I'm still exhausted and we have returned to face to face teaching.

***

From Emma McKenzie, early childhood teacher, Australia

The children kept me going. It is a privilege to be able to learn and work alongside a young child, and make a positive difference in their life. I love the innocence of childhood and their natural positivity and enthusiasm. My focus during the pandemic was to ensure their wellbeing was looked after. Children have a naturally positive and innocent outlook on life, so they were therapeutic for me and I tried to maintain a 'norm' for them, despite the frightening things they were hearing on the news. We talked openly and honestly about what was taking place, but tried to stick to routines and maintain a certain normalcy.

***

From a middle school teacher, New South Wales

I felt under pressure watching my colleagues adapt unbelievably fast and master the new technology. Maybe it was in my head but it felt like we were on two sides – the 'yes we can do this and adapt' and the 'what just happened – I don't like it this way' sides. I felt clueless and left behind – like I was the slowest to figure it all out. On the up side, I did learn a lot of things I can use from now on. I just wish there was an adjustment time. We didn't get that. It was 'bang – this is what we're doing and we're starting everything now.' Maybe if we had a week just to process what was happening around the world without the pressure to keep teaching. I could have got a lot more from the learning curve if things went a little slower. Maybe it's just me. . . .

To close, Educators know that whatever they felt there was someone else, somewhere in the world, feeling just like them. We are never alone in our troubles. Whatever you felt back then and now is perfectly okay and, yes, it matters.

2 Resetting for healthy wellbeing

In the sting of a setback, or an indigestible week, the easiest reset button might feel like 'run.' Escape the frustration, don't think about it and urge things back to 'normal' as soon as possible. Yet every setback, crisis or challenge impacts your life in a way; there is no return to exactly 'how it was.' Resetting your thinking and daily habits is inevitable and necessary sometimes. During a reset, you instigate a review of what is and isn't working, creating new and potentially better routines. You also think outside the square.

Resetting shouldn't be limited to setbacks, crises and major life events. A career in Education provides high job satisfaction, right alongside high pressure. The significant physical, mental and emotional contribution that being an Educator requires calls upon the need for a daily, or at the very least weekly, reset. Allowing time for personal resets to uplift your wellbeing will help keep you motivated and energised throughout your career in a job that is much more than a job, it's a calling. The added bonus is often an increase in productivity, freeing up time to enjoy more of what you need personally, not just professionally.

You will find plenty of ideas in this chapter to reset your thoughts, feelings and energy levels. Some are one-off endeavours, to swiftly improve your wellbeing and self-awareness. Others take more time and practice. Find what resonates with you, and choose one or two at a time to trial for as long as you need. Stay closely tuned in to how the strategies are helping you feel, and pay attention to the ripple effect they are having on all aspects of your life and relationships. Some tools are easier than others and not all of them will suit you right now. *Educator Wellbeing* is a framework honouring that you are indeed the expert in your life, and only you can make the final decisions on what you can and can't do right now.

Look for possibilities

There are doubtlessly many obstacles that intercept your daily wellbeing. Being an Educator is just one of many important roles you manoeuvre. Through sheer exhaustion from a heavy physical, mental and emotional load, engaging in wellbeing practices can easily feel unachievable. A more palatable reset solution that tempts many of us is scrolling through social media or binge-watching your favourite television series while diving into a bowl (or glass) of something delicious.

While switching off this way is relatively benign in the scheme of habits you could fall into, too much of this style of resetting can inhibit and stagnate you long term. When you switch off in ways that are designed to numb or distract from your feelings, those feelings might disappear for a while, but return eventually – usually with a vengeance.

Nurturing a hopeful, strengths-based 'possibility' mindset will help lead you towards a healthier wellbeing path. Investing time into making wellbeing possible, despite the obstacles, is your way forward. Take a moment to answer the following 'possibilities' questions:

> Where do you have space in your work day for a two-minute wellbeing reset practice?
> Can you find another space in your day for an additional two-minute wellbeing practice?

I've chosen two minutes, because even the busiest person on earth can find two minutes a day for self-care. If you can't, you probably need this book way more than you first realised!

Two minutes is a start. The idea is to spend a lot more time on your daily wellbeing. This will happen more intuitively once you start to feel and see the ripple effect it has on every aspect of your life, increasing your motivation to make yourself a priority without feeling guilty or overwhelmed.

> What is something you already enjoy as an Educator that supports your wellbeing?
> Is there a colleague, friend or partner who might join you in a wellbeing practice?
> What wellbeing tools do you like that are most accessible to you?

Keeping your mind open to possibilities will sometimes feel harder than focusing on obstacles. Don't be hard on yourself; this comes part and parcel with being a tired human. Making excuses and focusing on why you can't do something is a common default position for most of us – funnily enough, especially when our wellbeing is low.

If you don't have any wellbeing ideas yet, don't worry, that's what this book is for. In that case, return to these questions at a later date, once you've delved deeper into these pages.

Where are you thriving? Where are you stagnating?

Not often do we pause and reflect on where we're thriving and what's already working in our lives. It's somehow easier to employ a deficit view of what isn't working or what you still want to achieve. When you fail to acknowledge and celebrate your successes, you're likely to feel less valuable and your wellbeing is often the first to suffer. Acknowledging what's going well in your work as an Educator can build your confidence and help you take realistic and constructive action that benefits all aspects of your life. Consciously noticing what isn't working is also valuable, so you know what needs reducing or deleting. Just be cautious that you don't give this more weight than is useful or necessary.

Imagine how much better you might feel if you ended each work day focusing on where you're thriving and how far you've already come in Education, instead of where you're struggling and how much you have to do tomorrow.

Take a moment to answer the following reset questions:

1   *What is already working in your career right now?/Where are you thriving?*
    (Write it down, acknowledge it, appreciate and celebrate it.)
    Keep doing these as long as they continue to be helpful and constructive to you.

2   *What isn't working in your career right now?/What is a heavy weight on your Educator shoulders?*
    (Write it down, acknowledge it, take caution to it.)
    Stop or reduce your exposure to this. Ask for your supporters to help you if necessary.

3   *What do you want to start doing as an Educator that you think will help you reset and support your wellbeing?*
    (Write it down in order of how easy it is to start.)
    Start one step at a time. Choose the easiest reset practice and take one small step at a time towards it.

These questions are simple, yet how often do we bring them to conscious awareness? Answering questions like these, then taking action on them, is crucial for sustainable wellbeing. They allow you to tailor a unique, self-driven and personal wellbeing reset approach that's consistent with your own experience of life in Education.

Celebrate your achievements and validate your progress

Educators are adaptable, creative and resilient folk. You cleverly create learning opportunities that allow for daily 'micro-wins' that contribute to a young person's long-term, big wins. I've rarely known Educators to take the time to celebrate their own wins and achievements. This is partly because they often have personalities that naturally go above and beyond the call of duty and also because there's often little time or energy left in the day to pause and celebrate – unless you make it a priority. Maybe celebrating your wins becomes what you consciously focus your mind on as you commute home from work each night.

Until you learn to do otherwise, human nature has a tendency to spend more time thinking about the past and worrying about the future than celebrating how far we have come, what's going well and enjoying the moment of arrival, in front of you.

> What are five achievements, no matter how small, that you have had in the last seven days in your role as an Educator?
> What are five bigger achievements as an Educator that you're proud of during your career?
> Is it worthwhile opening a dialogue with your team about how acknowledging and celebrating Educator wins could be incorporated into staff meetings or lunch room conversations once a week?

Get comfortable with discomfort and struggle

Life in Education rarely follows a linear path. Working with a diverse group of children and adults means that discomfort and struggle are a common experience. Learning how to sit with discomfort and struggle isn't easy. People naturally have the tendency to move away from it or wish it away.

Part of resetting your mind is learning to fully experience discomfort. The benefit to your wellbeing when you learn to sit with this kind of struggle is that you come face to face with your emotions and practice responding to and handling them consciously. Each time you do this, you become more used to coping this way; you deepen your self-awareness and strengthen your emotional intelligence.

Learning to sit with discomfort and struggle is usually hard to execute. Be patient with yourself as you learn this tool. To build a more constructive response to uncomfortable feelings and struggle, you sit with the discomfort. You let it exist. You acknowledge what you're feeling and thinking. You allow yourself to feel things fully.

Meeting discomfort and struggle with resistance, on the other hand, will only make things more intense. Sometimes, it will mean you distract yourself from it and feel okay for a while . . . but it always comes back one way or another.

> Write down everything that makes you feel uncomfortable about your role as an Educator.
> Name the challenges you're struggling with right now in your environment.

Did the length of your list surprise you? My list was full when I did the same task at the start of the Global Pandemic. In amongst my intense sadness for the health, wellbeing and economy of our beautiful world, I was simultaneously watching my keynotes and speaking engagements be cancelled, our group programmes – the backbone of our business – get postponed indefinitely, our practice's revenue drop by over three quarters, while running costs continued . . . all the while, raising a young family who needed me to be vigilant *and* calm. Getting comfortable with uncomfortable was easier said than done. Educators had a whole other layer as well: 'Just keep going, folks, do whatever it takes for your students.'

Now that you have consciously identified what makes you uncomfortable, going from easiest discomfort to process to hardest, number your list (with one being easiest to 'sit with' and ten being hardest to 'sit with'). Starting with the easiest (number one), plan to allow all your feelings to be present, without distracting yourself from them, next time you're in that situation.

Remember, this doesn't come naturally to anyone who hasn't been taught this yet, so take your time with it and forgive yourself if you can't manage it. You can always try again later.

Getting comfortable with uncomfortable: a framework

1. Be prepared ahead of time. Know what pushes your buttons.
2. Plan to face the situation consciously and face the emotions courageously.
3. The situation occurs.
4. Notice and name the feelings it brings.
5. Allow the feelings in.
6. Be brave enough to feel your feelings.
7. Stop anytime you like. It will get easier to handle discomfort for longer, every time you practice it.
8. If you like, use your journal to write down your experience. Some people have a supportive person they can talk to and prefer this to journaling.

A word of caution

Everyone's circumstances are different. The process of allowing uncomfortable feelings without distraction can feel overwhelming. You know yourself better than anyone else. You know your life and your tolerance levels, based on that life. If you don't feel ready to do this, or don't have the support you need to get through this, come back to this practice at a later date. Or leave it out completely. You don't have to use every tool in *Educator Wellbeing* to improve your wellbeing. Not all the strategies are suitable for everyone.

Remember to start from the easiest struggle and don't stay immersed in the struggle longer than is necessary or healthy. For some, a good time is as short as a minute. For others, you might be ready to tolerate this for five minutes or longer. This is an exercise in self-awareness, not a saboteur of your thoughts and feelings for the day.

Reset with healthy methods to respond to difficulty

By healthy methods, I mean ways that aren't harmful to you or others. Difficult situations lead to difficult feelings. If you don't know what to do about difficult feelings, it's very possible you will take them out on yourself, or others. While it's okay to fall in a heap sometimes and mismanage your self-care a little, habitual responses to difficulty that involve conflict with yourself and others, over eating or engaging in addictive behaviours will inevitably damage your wellbeing.

Allow time for grief, sadness, frustration and worry about what you've faced. As uncomfortable as they feel, they are part of the process of adjusting. You're human; you're meant to feel deeply.

Once you've acknowledged and accepted your feelings, to help ease the discomfort and move those feelings through, you might like to try something to help you feel better. Some ways that can be helpful include:

- Talk openly to a loved one about how you're really feeling. Get it all out in every detail.
- Write your experiences, thoughts and feelings in a journal, every day.
- Find reasons to feel hopeful. What is okay in your life right now? What can you look forward to?
- Remember happier times. Reflect on great memories. Bring them back into your mind. Talk about them with your loved ones.
- Learn breathing, presence and mindfulness techniques.
- Play music you love in your home more often.
- Look at art. Create art. Appreciate art.
- Watch, listen to and read things that make you feel upbeat enough to smile and laugh.
- Play. Have fun for the sake of fun.
- Look at nature and experience nature.
- Find ways for regular movement.
- Choose as many fresh, whole foods as you can.

What can you add to this list to help move your difficult feelings through in healthy ways?

Start asking yourself 'what could go right?' when you're worried about taking a calculated risk or making a decision

A healthy wellbeing reset tool when you're met with a setback or feeling uncertain is to ask yourself, 'what could go right?' You don't have to be feeling optimistic to apply this thought. You don't even have to believe it's possible anything *will* go right. By allowing this thought into your mind, you're welcoming hope. With that hope, you might see some possibilities that build courage and new ways.

Try and avoid cultivating, resisting and rehearsing your upsets

While all that may sound complicated at first glance, it's not. I will explain each of them shortly. One of our great assets to wellbeing, is reaching emotional freedom. Untying ourselves as much as possible from the mental and emotional burdens we carry. We all have emotional bruises. Some bigger than others. We all experience worry. Some more often than others. We all struggle to process and tether these in ways that are supportive to our wellbeing. Educators know these challenges all too well.

Struggling with challenges like these is exactly what it means to be human. We think. We feel. We react and respond. The challenge it brings is, for each setback we carry a tendency to mull it over and again, usually far beyond what's necessary to make safe passage through it. Knowing how to reset your thoughts at the end of each day will not only promote your wellbeing but gives you a much better chance at a restful evening and a good night's sleep.

Let's start with how easily you can find yourself 'cultivating' unhelpful thoughts. When something goes wrong as an Educator, it's only natural for this to become the predominant thought in your mind. You go over it many times and it starts threading deeper and deeper into your thinking, cultivating the growth of uncomfortable thoughts about the difficult experience.

While it's only natural to dedicate thoughts to what you go through each day, it becomes unhelpful when you reach a point of fixation and get stuck in that singular thought. Often, you will add unnecessary details along the way, making it even more intense. This is how one bad experience can get cultivated further in your mind, upsetting you long after the event has been and gone.

Next may come resistance. This is where you might find yourself engaged in thoughts along the theme of 'why is work in Education thankless?' and 'why aren't I making progress with this student/class?' Again, these are completely natural responses to a challenge. If you stay too long here, however, you may find that you begin to turn too far inward, forgetting you're not the only Educator experiencing difficulty. Adversity is part of working in a complex role that involves not only matters of the mind, but matters of the heart. Education settings are full of ups, downs and twists in the road. Getting stuck in resistance about what happened in your class or school can lead to hopelessness and throw your wellbeing into a spin. As long as you're resisting what's bothering you, you're arguing with reality.

Finally, there's the habit of 'rehearsing.' People tend to go over what happened to upset them more times than is necessary in taking the lesson and moving forward. What follows may be an onslaught of thoughts about everything that could subsequently happen because of the upset . . . what you think people might say and do . . . what you might say and do . . . and what might happen to you long term because of this. All the while, the moment in front of you is slipping by with all the 'what ifs' and worst-case scenarios.

Rehearsal of the future and replay of past events can certainly help in the short term as we process information and plan solutions. Getting stuck there means an assault on your wellbeing with heavy and unhelpful thoughts that inhibit you from resting, playing, talking, moving, loving, laughing and nourishing your wellbeing.

So how you do get unstuck from cultivating, resisting and rehearsing? An awareness of these tendencies is the first and most essential step. Simply knowing this is a thinking trap that many people spend their life in a habitual rollercoaster on is the start of resolving to new ways.

Try identifying and building healthier stress response behaviours like journaling, talking to someone, cultivating hope, non-judgementally accepting what's happened and doing your best to stay present and mindful. You'll find plenty more ways to respond to this kind of thinking throughout this book.

Adjust your expectations of yourself and others

When challenges, unexpected changes, crises or even grief occur, there's an overall sense of urgency to 'get back on track' and return to 'life as usual' as quickly as possible. All that most of us want is for the horrible experience to go away. It's so painful to sit with it and give it the time of day.

It's not possible for anything to return to exactly how it was after you've experienced something upsetting, disruptive and perhaps life-changing. No matter how much you miss the old way, you can't stride back into it as if nothing has changed. Not without some serious consequences down the track anyway.

When life is a little tangled, you won't have the luxury of your usual levels of resilience. If you were already vulnerable and experiencing hardship, anxiety, depression and stress, a new layer of challenge may mean you're now just barely hanging on.

After life altering events and even a period of moderate challenge, you're entitled to adjust your expectations, to cut yourself some slack and be less confident and productive than usual. Your students who are struggling deserve the same grace, too. A culture of unrealistic expectations can be contagious and overwhelming. Creating a flexible and compassionate culture of understanding, patience and forgiveness can happen when everyone contributes to the movement.

Doing your own small part in keeping expectations of yourself as an Educator and others as students and co-workers realistic and fair will have a strong ripple effect on the culture around you. It's also important to remember that no one really knows fully what someone else might be going through. Wellbeing is not static, so even with nothing notable going on, a colleague, friend or family member may be suffering their own private battle and cannot sustain their usual standards of communication and behaviour.

Allow yourself to 'feel the feels' and experience some anxiety

It's normal to experience some anxiety. Our body warns us when something isn't quite right and we might need to be alert and take action. It does this through feelings like anxiety. When you're experiencing a genuine worry or your Education setting changes rapidly and you're experiencing uncertainty, anxiety is a healthy physiological response and 'cry for help.'

Anxiety has been disparaged to some degree in the happiness movement. There's almost a new flavour of anxiety today – anxiety about anxiety. Yet anxiety is necessary for keeping you on track and aware of what is and isn't working. Certainly when it impacts on your quality of life in destructive ways, then you must seek help, but generally speaking, a little anxiety is part and parcel of responding to life not being completely in our control.

During the Global Pandemic everything changed dramatically. Few people had time and space to feel the intensity of the blow and had to simply keep going. Educators were part of this group that had to respond quickly, creatively and diligently. There was little time to process the anxiety it came with.

Next time you're anxious (or if you're still anxious after a past event), allow yourself time to face it, acknowledge it and then give it safe passage. There are many tools to support you and they start with healthy wellbeing practices like help seeking, talking, writing, moving, playing, watching funny things, reading, listening to your favourite music, embracing nature, resting and whatever is good for your own personal wellbeing. If anxiety is impacting on your ability to engage with and enjoy most aspects of your life, then perhaps it's time to seek professional support. Anxiety is not a sign of weakness and asking for help is only ever a sign of courage.

Don't be hard on yourself for feeling anxious sometimes. To feel anxious in response to difficulty is part of being human.

Identify and prepare for what pushes your buttons

Educators will naturally have student behaviours that push their buttons. When buttons have been pushed, it's hard to respond calmly. When you're resetting your emotional resilience, knowing what bothers you in a student, class or colleague, and having a plan to respond, can help you face tricky situations with more confidence. Let's say you're agitated by student dishonesty. Acknowledge the feeling, accept it and plan a response for the next time you see a student being dishonest. You can't control what your others do from one day to the next, but you can improve how you manage your own thoughts, feelings and reactions when they don't behave as well as they could.

- What behaviour pushes your buttons?
- What expectations in Education push your buttons?
- What classroom dynamics push your buttons?
- What helps you calm down when your buttons have been pushed?
- What are some positive self-talk statements (like 'I am calm' or 'I can handle this') that might help you calm your thinking and not lead to a reaction when your buttons are pushed?
- What are some ways to respond (like moving away, stating your boundaries, regulating your breathing or finding a peaceful focal point) that you could apply when your buttons have been pushed?

Grow familiar with the situations you're agitated by so when your enter them you do so with self-awareness and focus; regulate your feelings responsibly. Next time you find yourself provoked, increased self-awareness and careful planning give you the best chance to stay calm and to respond in a thoughtful manner. Emotional regulation takes conscious effort and practice before it becomes routine; it can benefit your wellbeing. It is infinitely harder in Education because young people are still learning and tend to be emotionally reactive, which means more of your buttons are likely to get pushed, and there tends to be a natural contagion of emotion.

Time to move on. Forgive yourself. Forgive others, ask for forgiveness

Many Educators and others in essential services felt forgotten during the Global Pandemic of 2020. Some of these feelings were not given time to process the high expectations placed on these workers that kept everyone on their toes with little time for reflection and growth. Holding on to unforgiving feelings can lead to toxic levels of anger and have a negative impact on your stress levels, affecting your cardiac and psychological health (Chida & Steptoe, 2009).

The wellbeing aspects of forgiveness include its link to mental health outcomes such as reduced anxiety, depression and major psychiatric disorders, as well as experiencing fewer physical health symptoms and lower mortality rates (Toussaint, Worthington and Williams 2015). When a person has the skills to forgive and reduce toxic anger, their muscles relax, they feel less anxious, they have more energy and their immune system can strengthen.

Forgiveness can feel rocky, but making the conscious decision to work towards forgiveness is a step to better wellbeing, so you have the best chance at resetting without more emotional baggage than you can navigate.

To forgive someone doesn't mean you automatically excuse what they have done, give up your boundaries or uncomfortably befriend them. You simply work towards accepting what has happened, assuming their actions were the best they could offer with the skills, knowledge and awareness they had at the time. This compassionate recognition of their position might be the last thing you feel like doing, but it's an important step to take when you're ready.

The more you practice letting go of other people's actions, the better for your personal health and wellbeing. Toxic anger will hurt you more than the person who hurt you. Remember that students rarely intentionally upset you. They are young, inexperienced and some have experienced trauma, family upsets or grapple with neurobiological challenges that mean they can't behave well a lot of the time. When they are emotionally dysregulated, they will struggle to think reasonably. These students need our understanding and forgiveness. From there, they are better equipped to connect with you and grow.

Cultivate feelings you want more of

While it's unrealistic to experience comfortable and peaceful emotions all the time, research by Barbara Fredrickson (2000) shows you can cultivate positive emotions to uplift and balance your wellbeing.

> What are your most favoured feelings as an Educator? Pride? Satisfaction? Pleasure? Connection? Accomplishment?

Choose one feeling each week that you want to cultivate. To help you remember your plan to cultivate the feeling, you may write it down and display it somewhere you can see it every day. Then take the following steps:

- In a quiet moment, perhaps as you're waking in the morning, bring your feeling to mind.
- Think of ways you can do something as an Educator that will bring about that feeling in you.
- Make a conscious effort to do what you planned.
- Whenever you feel that feeling, acknowledge its presence, savour it and enjoy it. Make it meaningful and connect it with your students by telling them what you're feeling. For example, you might say, 'I feel so proud when I walk into the classroom and see you all getting organised without being asked.'

Learning to consciously welcome favourable feelings is an investment in your wellbeing that has far reaching benefits to you and the people connected with you.

Reset and build your emotional intelligence to welcome a broad range of emotions and experiences

Emotional intelligence is essential for getting along with others and sustaining healthy and balanced relationships. While you won't necessarily earn a certificate that shows you are emotionally intelligent, like you might for an academic or sporting achievement, emotional intelligence grounds you for long term connection with others. Becoming emotionally intelligent is a process and involves many factors including practicing empathy and emotional regulation.

Take a moment to reflect on how you respond to your feelings in your role as an Educator and how you intuitively feel you're fairing on the emotional intelligence front. The following step by step framework can be adapted to your personal situation and offers you a guideline to embrace and adjust adaptively to a broad range of feelings and experiences:

1 *Feelings awareness:* Learn to pay attention to your feelings. When feelings arise, practice asking yourself, 'What am I feeling?' Naming your feelings is an integral part of handling emotions constructively.
2 *Feelings acceptance:* Accept your feelings – they visit for a reason. They might be telling you something isn't right and needs your attention. Alternatively, they might be telling you your thinking needs re-thinking. Wishing them away or fighting them won't work no matter how hard you try.
3 *Do something with your feelings:* Do something helpful with uncomfortable feelings to help you think clearly again. You might need to get moving or slow down. Either way, meet your emotions with something useful.

4   *Pay attention to other people's feelings:* Notice what other people feel. Are they frustrated? Jealous? Angry? Sad? Accept their feelings even if you don't agree with them. They are allowed to have their emotions. Doing this shows empathy. Empathy builds emotional intelligence (and healthy relationships).
5   *Welcome other people's thoughts and feelings:* Respectfully welcome (or at the very least, acknowledge and accept) other people's opinions, thoughts and feelings. You don't have to agree to be friendly. If this gets hard, try imagining how you might feel if you were them and saw things their way.
6   *Communicate and behave calmly:* Talk and behave in understanding, non-judgemental and respectful ways. If you don't know how to do this or find this confusing, take the time to invest in learning how. (This book is a great starting point.)
7   *Be compassionate about other people's feelings:* Be caring and helpful when a student is upset or going through a tough time. This is known as 'compassion.' If you're too upset, go back to steps 1, 2 and 3 to slow down. If your feelings take over and you do something hurtful, do what you can to make things better with the person. Be kind to them and to yourself.

With strong emotional intelligence, your wellbeing can flourish without the burden of heavy, unbridled and unsupported thoughts and feelings. You can come out more emotionally strong and healthy than you went in to any challenge.

The compassion reset when you don't see eye to eye

Consistently getting along with others harmoniously is a multi-faceted, social and emotional intelligence skill. With so many different temperaments in the classroom community, there will always be challenges arising between personalities. It's unrealistic to expect everyone to feel agreeable all the time. The challenge this presents to your state of wellbeing is when you meet a student's opposing nature with resistance, anger and frustration. You inevitably find yourself in a state of agitation, affecting your mood and ability to feel emotionally balanced.

Engaging in a compassionate exercise, like the one here, is one way to build compassion for people you don't find easy to communicate with or be around. It's also one you can teach your students.

> Think of a student you have trouble understanding or getting along with. It might be one who has strong opinions different from yours, or even a student who is rude to you. Once you've chosen a student, the goal is to spend some time each day trying to see the world through their eyes. How are you different? How might you be similar? What strengths do you see in the young person? Why might they behave or speak the way they do? You might like to extend yourself further to try and get to know them even better. Smile at them, talk to them, and, if you can, find a way to give them a compliment. As you do this, allow a little time each day to notice what you are learning about this student in the process.

This activity works just as well if you're struggling with a colleague or someone in your personal life.

Play around with your routine

While sameness can feel comforting, you can also reset and energise your wellbeing by adding some simple changes to your daily routine like:

- Playing music while having a shower.
- Eating breakfast outdoors (or indoors if you normally eat outdoors!).
- Taking a slightly different route to work.
- Imagining you're a tourist and paying a new kind of attention to your school.
- Buying groceries somewhere out of your neighbourhood.
- Learning a new skill or Google a topic you know nothing about.

Introducing planned changes like these can bring a sense of adventure and uplift your everyday routine.

Accept your thoughts and feelings without judgement

Healthy wellbeing relies on being kind enough to yourself so that you're not judging harshly and unreasonably how you think and feel. While it's important to be self-aware and notice the patterns of your thoughts and feelings, it's also important to acknowledge the automaticity of thoughts and feelings. Our healthy wellbeing and emotional intelligence need our thoughts and feelings to be responded to in healthy ways. Next time you experience a challenging thought or feeling, accept it without judgement. When judgement creeps in (because it will), reset, accept and don't judge yourself.

> Make a list of thoughts and feelings you've been harshly judging.
> Take a moment to pause and accept them without judgement.

No one has a perfect and consistent stream of healthy and confident thoughts and feelings.

Learn to deal with the moment in front of you

How quickly minds race ahead after an obstacle with 'what if.' We create stories in our minds to make sense of everything and soothe the unknown. Often this will involve 'stabs in the dark,' imagining worst-case scenarios. No one can ever know for certain what is happening tomorrow – or even in the next moment. Work in Education requires a resiliency to lack of certainty, predictability and the absence of formulaic solutions.

Racing ahead or looking back is a luxury you can't afford in a job that requires you do so much thinking on the spot. The only moment you can have impact on is the moment in front of you. While planning ahead as an Educator is important and responsible, planning that isn't founded in truth and is based on anxiety can tip your wellbeing completely out of balance.

When you find your mind drifting ahead with worry, try and bring it back to the present. Use a wellbeing technique from this book or of your own to help settle and soothe your feelings. If you need to, take one constructive step forward, no matter how small, to respond to your challenge, then take a break until you're ready for the next step. When you struggle to do this, be kind and forgiving to yourself. No one finds this easy until they have had enough time and practice doing it.

One way to practice being in the moment is by taking a mindful walk. Try keeping your mind focused solely on the act of walking. Soak in the surroundings in front of you, consciously taking it all in. Feel your feet hitting the ground one foot a time. When your mind drifts ahead or into the past, bring it back into the experience of walking. Keep practicing being present like this every day. In time, this will become more natural and invaluably available to you next time you're faced with a challenge. While you can't just take a mindful walk in the middle of a school day, practicing this tool outside of your teaching time gets you more used to staying in the moment. You will find plenty more mindfulness and presence techniques later in this book.

Fire and wire wellbeing thoughts

The most frequently used thoughts will build the most robust neurological pathways in your brain. These pathways become our thinking habits, and our thinking habits affect the nature of our feelings (Hanson 2016).

> Create some reminders to cultivate optimism and a wellbeing mindset. You can come up with your own or use the ones here for inspiration:
>
> - I have fellow Educators who empathise and care about me.
> - I am healthy.
> - I am a capable Educator.
> - My work is making a difference, even if I don't receive thanks very often.
> - I educate with integrity.
> - I do my best for my students and my school.
> - I am kind and compassionate.
> - I belong in Education.
> - I'm irreplaceable.
>
> Continue to choose healthy, helpful and optimistic thoughts as much as possible.

Find a circuit breaker when feelings get challenging

When you're feeling upset sometimes it's hard to think about anything else. A circuit breaker can help get you out of a worry loop through a distraction. It might be turning on music, a change of scenery, taking a drink of water, opening a window or calling a friend to see how they are.

Using a focal point as a circuit breaker

Paying attention to a focal point nearby is also a way to distract yourself from your thoughts and feelings. Focal points might be a tree outside your classroom, a candle at your desk, a painting . . . anything pleasant or neutral to look at.

When you notice your mind wandering or becoming negative and anxious, find your focal point, then describe it mentally in detail. When challenging thoughts and feelings return, revisit your focal point. Many Educators find it easier to calm down this way than by generating and sustaining positive thoughts. It isn't always possible in a busy classroom, but it's a good 'go to' strategy when your students are occupied and your mind is struggling with something.

The heartbeat, pulse or breath as a focal point

Your pulse, breathing rate and heartbeat are your own personal, portable focal points. Finding a pulse and concentrating on it, touching your chest to feel your heart beating or attending to your breathing are all focal points that can help you return to the present and manage difficult feelings. Teaching your students to do this is a great way of bringing this wellbeing practice into the classroom environment and extending its benefit beyond yourself. Next time your class is struggling (and you are too as a result), think about resetting and connecting by taking a moment to monitor your heartbeat, pulse or breath.

Understand stress and reset the ways you handle it

Stress triggers our primitive 'fight or flight' response giving a strong burst of adrenalin. Uncomfortable feelings follow suit. The physiological aspect of stress can feel frightening when you don't understand what is happening. Adrenalin gives extra energy that can either be used for 'fight' (problem solving, solution seeking, physical exertion for stress relief) or 'flight' (avoiding the problem, keeping it cycling around in your head), or in some situations, 'freeze' (doing nothing and becoming paralysed with stress). Understanding your stress response and developing useful methods to calm it creates neural pathways for coping. With practice these pathways become stronger and easier to use.

Education is one of those careers where stress is inevitable – that's why it's not for the faint-hearted. An Educator who can handle stress well is bound for better wellbeing and resilience with higher emotional intelligence up their sleeve. *Educator Wellbeing* is packed with ways to be proactive and responsive to stress.

Know your body and respond to what it's telling you

Feelings happen in your mind and body – at the same time. Your body's reaction can vary depending on what you're going through at the time and how resilient you are feeling. Understanding exactly how your body reacts helps you navigate and respond to feelings proactively. Physiological changes in your body are 'early warning signs' that you're struggling and healthy action needs to be taken.

Next time you're upset by a situation with a student, colleague or your class, try to pay attention to what your body does. Do a quick body scan and acknowledge the sensations. Drawing conscious awareness to the physical aspect of your feelings is essential for developing your emotional intelligence and growing from what your feelings are trying to tell you.

Reset the need for your 'big break' and value the small steps

For most Educators, there are no 'big breaks.' When you experience a career or personal breakthrough, it's usually a result of many years of small, constructive steps. These micro steps need to be individually acknowledged and valued. Your wellbeing and confidence is strengthened when you are able to focus on how far you've come and hold a willingness to continue making small steps towards reaching your goals. Don't look for or wait for the 'big break.' As long as you're waiting for something big to happen, you are miles from the present and missing the opportunity to acknowledge, celebrate and appreciate all the small steps and little breaks that got you to where you are right now. You will also waste your time in a state of inadequacy instead of fulfillment.

Reset to respond, instead of react, by being quiet when you're upset (unless it's absolutely necessary)

Emotions are great teachers. They let you know very clearly what you do and don't like. While they need to be noticed, acknowledged and accepted, they also need tethering sometimes. Learning not to act in the heat of emotion takes time, conscious effort and practice. Educators need to develop this skill, as a day spent with young, developing minds inevitably means there will be behaviours and emotions that push your buttons.

Try making a conscious daily attempt to not act on emotion or impulse. Making this intention is the first step you need to take. Before you start work, try telling yourself to respond to challenges only when you're calm.

> Make a list of all the things you tend to react emotionally to in your classroom.
> Imagine yourself in those situations – calm and balanced in your responses.
> Each time you're about to enter those situations, see yourself ahead of time responding calmly.

This takes practice so don't be hard on yourself if things don't go according to plan. Becoming aware of and planning for what pushes your buttons is, in itself, a leap forward.

For the times you find yourself acting on emotion and impulse, forgive yourself, write about it, talk about it and if it involved another person, ask how you can make it better.

You're human. You're allowed to make mistakes and be imperfect.

Reset to focus on connection, empathy and mutual respect

Your school community can flourish with healthy wellbeing when there is a strong and consistent commitment to the values of connection, empathy and mutual respect.

See what good you can gather together with your collective hearts and minds. You're all uniquely gifted and different. Our shared experience of humanity has the potential to make each of us stronger. This is how you each add value to your education setting. Stay connected with colleagues through the shared experience of being an Educator. Empathise with each other's challenges, even if you don't relate to them. Show mutual respect by allowing each other to work according to your own style without judging either way as 'right or wrong.'

All workplaces can be connected, empathic and respectful places, but not if there's guilt and judgement . . . not if there's division about what the right and wrong way to do things is.

Take a moment to close your eyes and think of a student or colleague you don't naturally see eye to eye with.

> Is there way you feel connected to them? A shared strength or difficulty?
> Can you take a moment to put yourself in their shoes and see life from where they are coming from?
> Can you find somewhere in your heart to respect them without judgement, to allow them to be who they are without wishing they would change?

When you open your eyes, remember you may well have been in the mind of someone who struggles with you. We all have our differences. Individuals are stronger in a united and mutually respectful group, so when you can, do everything possible to connect, empathise and show mutual respect. This strengthens your own sense of wellbeing as much as theirs. When dynamics are complex, your boundaries are important. Just stay neutral if connection, empathy and mutual respect are too challenging for now.

Want the best and wish the best for yourself

Culturally, Education is a career where professionals tend to be expected to put others (their students) before themselves, doing whatever it takes to support the wellbeing and growth of another person. Unintentionally, it is not unusual to see a culture of expectation where Educators must do whatever it takes to support their students and please parents and carers.

I often hear Educators tell me the reason they don't make time for themselves to engage in self-care (after the obvious – that they are working so hard) is that it evokes feelings of guilt and self-indulgence – like they shouldn't take a break or invest in themselves.

Educator wellbeing is a necessity. We need our Educators to be okay. When they are okay, they can carry out this vital work without burning out. When they are okay, their students feel it too. The ripple effect of strong Educator wellbeing cannot be underestimated.

Here's something new for your morning routine, either before you get out of bed or before you walk into your classroom. Wish yourself the best for the day ahead. Wish yourself happiness, fulfillment, joy, growth, connection, progress – whatever you want the most for yourself. Then take this wish into your heart and mind and repeat three times,

'May I be_____,' 'may I be _____,' 'may I be _____.'

See if you can repeat this wish for yourself every day without feeling guilty or indulgent. You are important, valuable and deserve the best of days.

Avoid taking other people's opinions or outcomes with students personally

This is hard. No matter what is said about not worrying what others think of you, we are social beings who seek connection and acceptance. While we can all learn to be less reliant on other people's opinions and be content with our integrity, most people will agree, if someone criticises you, it's hard not to feel hurt.

What other people say, do or think of you is completely out of your control. As long as you are keeping a heart and mind that's honest, gentle and kind (or at the very least, neutral), other people's opinions are just that, opinions.

When it comes to Education, another challenge is taking student progress personally. Working with young people is not an exact science. There are many psychological, developmental and learning variables at play. The fruits of your efforts one year may not show up in that student until the next year – or maybe even for years to come.

When you enter this work, you know you have strengths to deliver excellence. You arrive willing to put your heart, mind and soul into leading your students. That is your duty in a nutshell. To carry out your work with honesty, effort and creativity. I've seen Educators come up with the most inspiring ways to reach and teach their students. I've also seen for some, that no matter how many angles they've taken, they haven't been able to reach every young person – not in a way that's visible, anyway. Underneath the surface of their most difficult students, a tiny seed and then another was planted for that young person to feel seen, heard and valued. As this young person had many other challenges at play, the fruits of their teacher, counsellor or school support officer's efforts was not visible, but one day it will be a huge contributing factor to their success.

Recognise that your student's academic, social or emotional growth is not entirely on your shoulders. You must not take the outcomes personally when you are working hard and doing your best. Talk to a colleague. Be open about the struggle. Enlist extra support when necessary and, remember, you're not a walking, talking magic wand.

Reduce your mental load by writing a 'to do' list

Educators are well known for carrying a sizeable mental load. Working with young people means there is always plenty to do right in front of you and a whole other layer of responsibility that you carry around in your mind, day in, day out.

The weight of a mental load is very real and can tax your wellbeing. Often, obligations feel more complicated and overwhelming when they're sailing about in our minds rather than transferring them onto paper – as you might on a 'to do' list. This way, when you have time to attend to them, you can look at your list and respond to what you can.

While this doesn't magically lift the enormity of your responsibilities, it does place them into a 'compartment' that is less likely to interrupt your night and day as all the loose ends come to mind, repeatedly and relentlessly.

Start with a small piece of paper and write your own 'to do' list. See if you feel better by getting it off your chest. In some ways, this is similar to journaling your thoughts and feelings but provides a separate place to release your daily tasks. Your mind can't reset if it is the keeper of not only your thoughts but also the keeper of your obligations. Your wellbeing matters and so much of your wellbeing is reliant on a peaceful and clear mind.

Build a growth mindset

Over 30 years ago, Carol Dweck coined the term 'growth mindset' to explain how abilities and intelligence can be developed through time, effort and hard work. A fixed mindset on the other hand is a belief that your intelligence and abilities are predetermined and you either 'have it' or you don't. A person with a growth mindset is more likely to persist and keep going because they're less worried about being 'smart' and getting things 'right' and their attention is instead on learning (Dweck 2012). Without a growth mindset, you're at risk of not growing to your full potential and seeing mistakes as permanent failings and signs of inner weakness and poor intelligence and capability. Children's beliefs become mental 'baggage' carried into learning situations. Negative experiences have lasting negative effects primarily when they affect an individual's beliefs (Dodge, Pettit, Bates and Valente 1995; Dweck and London 2004; Gibb et al. 2001).

What about Educators? Many Educators can benefit from using a growth mindset for their own wellbeing, to help them handle mistakes better, learn from challenges, be optimistic and persistent and, as a result, improve their capacity as an Educator (Blackwell, Trzesniewski and Dweck 2014).

Here are a handful of growth mindset thinking skills for Educators:

1 *Learn from your mistakes.*
   When you make a mistake ask yourself, 'what have I learnt that I can use next time I'm doing this?'

2 *Face yourself and be self-aware.*
   That means you get to know your strengths as well as your difficulties. Ask yourself, 'What is getting in the way of me using a growth mindset? What is stopping me?'

3 *Be curious.*
   Keep learning, find out more about students in your life, places you visit and things that interest you. Be a lifelong learner. Ask questions and listen to the answers.

4 *Be optimistic about your ability to handle challenges.*
   Learning and growing take a lot of time, effort and hard work. Tell yourself you can handle obstacles as well as the tough feelings that come with them.

5 *Be inspired instead of jealous.*
   It's easy to get caught up in comparisons and see other people's success as your failure. Next time you see another Educator doing well or doing something you wish you were doing, be inspired instead of jealous and think about how you can use this inspiration to continue growing. In the same way, you might like to see yourself as an Educator who can inspire others too.

6 *Embrace imperfection.*
   No one is perfect. When you receive feedback on something you could do differently or better – or you notice something for improvement in yourself, acknowledge it and tell yourself, 'I'm human.' Use these challenges as an opportunity for self-improvement.

7 *Choose your words.*
   The words you use will give you a feeling that can uplift you or pull you down. Instead of words like 'failing' try words like, 'learning,' 'growing,' 'thriving' and 'trying.'

8 *Learn well, not fast.*
   Be willing to wait for your growth and try not to rush your progress. Working hard is important but working too fast can reduce your learning.

9 *The power of 'yet.'*
   Carol Dweck has made the term 'not yet' famous for building a growth mindset. Next time you can't do something, say, 'I can't do that YET.'

10 *Be responsible for your own learning.*
   Take ownership of your progress and attitude. When learning gets hard it can be easy to blame others or circumstances for your struggle. While some things are out of your control, make sure you're taking full responsibility for how much effort you're putting in and be accountable.

Growth mindset thinking doesn't come naturally to most of us. Take time and be patient with yourself as you learn these tools that will nurture your wellbeing and allow you to be self-compassionate as you go through the ups and downs of your life as an Educator.

Final thoughts

Hitting reset is an important wellbeing tool. Finding what's suitable for you and using it at a time that's most effective for you personally takes careful consideration. There is no need to rush through any of these tools. Resetting takes time and a steady commitment, one day at a time.

References

Blackwell, S., Trzesniewski, H. and Dweck, C. (2007). Implicit Theories of Intelligence Predict Achievement Across an Adolescent Transition: A Longitudinal Study and an Intervention. *Child Development*, 78(1): 246–63.

Chida, Y. and Steptoe, A. (2009). The Association of Anger and Hostility with Future Coronary Heart Disease: A Meta-Analytic Review of Prospective Evidence. *Journal of the American College of Cardiology*, 53, 936–946.

Dodge, K. A., Pettit, G. S., Bates, J. E. and Valente, E. (1995). Social Information-Processing Patterns Partially Mediate the Effect of Early Physical Abuse on Later Conduct Problems. *Journal of Abnormal Psychology*, 104 (4), 632–643.

Dweck, C. (2012). *Mindset: How You Can Fulfill Your Potential*. London: Constable.

Dweck, C. and London, B. (2004). The Role of Mental Representation in Social Development. *Merrill-Palmer Quarterly*, 50(4), 428–444. DOI:10.1353/mpq.2004.0029.

Fredrickson, B. L. (2000, March 7). Prevention & Treatment, Volume 3, Article 0001a. Copyright 2000 by the American Psychological Association Cultivating Positive Emotions to Optimize Health and Well-Being Prevention & Treatment.

Gibb, B. E., Alloy, L. B., Abramson, L. Y., Rose, D. T., Whitehouse, W. G., Donovan, P., Hogan, M. E., Cronholm, J. and Tierney, S. (2001). History of Childhood Maltreatment, Negative Cognitive Styles, and Episodes of Depression in Adulthood. *Cognitive Therapy and Research*, 25 (4), 425–446.

Hanson, R. (2016). *Hardwiring Happiness: The New Brain Science of Contentment, Calm and Confidence*. New York: Harmony Publishing.

Toussaint, L., Worthington, E. and Williams, D. R. (2015). *Forgiveness and Health: Scientific Evidence and Theories Relating Forgiveness to Better Health*. Springer. DOI:10.1007/978-94-017-9993-5.

3 Recharging your wellbeing battery

Working with young people in Education takes ongoing physical, cognitive and emotional energy. While there is a sense of heaviness that comes with that statement, this investment is also the reason why your profession is exhilarating, enriching and brain tingling – in a good way.

There's a beautiful exchange that happens in Education where an adult stretches themselves far and wide to honour a young person's immediate and long-term growth. Your generous, daily investment powerfully impacts their trust and value in themselves and learning. The character you've helped build ripples down to their connections, now and well into their future. Educators are steady role models young people can look towards for balanced wisdom, compassion and leadership. By being yourself and investing in student connection so you can pass on your brilliance, you are making wonderful waves, big and small, long after your work with them has passed.

The recharge thinking tools, rituals and practices you're about to learn can help you feel strong, energised and alive, supporting you through your noble work. Take your time with finding not only what suits you personally, but is accessible and sustainable right now. Start with one idea, make it your own, see how it feels and make whatever next step is necessary. Add your own recharge ideas too. Find a way to make a daily recharge possible. The world needs you to continue sharing your gifts far and wide for as long as possible.

Recharge your self-talk: talk to yourself like you would talk to a treasured friend

If you sit for a moment, you'll notice the ongoing background chatter of your mind. It comes with a speed and automaticity that's hard to curate and subdue – especially when those thoughts are negative and critical. When you're met with a challenge, the nature of self-talk is often unhelpful, even hurtful. We can be quick to criticise ourselves unfairly. Negative self-talk can feel excruciatingly painful, draining your physical and emotional energy. It also feels very real – as if the thoughts are facts.

Take time to check in with the nature of your self-talk.

> Does it support your work as an Educator?
> Is it realistic given how many obligations you have in Education?
> Is it fair on you and how much effort you're putting into your job?

I know countless Educators who, under the pressure of the pandemic, felt frustrated with themselves for finding the transition to online learning (not to mention all the other changes) overwhelming and confusing. They could see colleagues adapting differently or quicker. They told me they felt mad at themselves a lot of the time and would catch themselves in the middle of negative banter that went back and forth in their mind, thoroughly exhausting them.

Your feelings are attached to your thoughts, so it's important for your wellbeing that you keep your thoughts, and in this case, your self-talk, in check.

One way to build more balanced self-talk is to talk to yourself with the same kindness and encouragement you would use with a treasured friend. Thoughts are going to enter your mind regardless. You can take the automatic ones, or you can consciously create ones that support you and focus on your strengths and abilities as an Educator. Be gentle with yourself by exchanging negative dialogue for optimistic and supportive thinking.

> What kind, understanding and caring things you tend to say to colleagues or others in Education when they come to you struggling with a student or classroom challenge?
> How do you help them feel better?

See yourself as a gentle, encouraging advisor to yourself, rather than a harsh, ongoing critic.

Clear your mind and learn to keep it clear, even amongst chaos

A clear mind is a valuable wellbeing tool in a busy school environment. You absorb the emotional climate around you, as part of the empathic exchange between people. As an Educator, you're in the unique situation of not only teaching but supporting emotional regulation when students are struggling. Only an Educator fully understands how quickly a classroom can go from calm and focused to dysregulated and disengaged.

If you don't declutter your daily thoughts and calm your mind, your wellbeing battery consumes fast. Each day you haven't recharged this way makes it harder the next day to keep a clear mind amongst the ups and downs of school life.

A helpful way to declutter your mind is by journaling your thoughts each evening until there's nothing left to write about. Some prefer to talk to someone and seek counsel or practice presence and mindfulness. Being active is another healthy way to clear your mind.

When you're surrounded by muddled thinking, consciously take on the role of being a quiet, non-judgemental observer to your thoughts. This helps you keep your mind less emotionally invested, clearer, more rational and balanced.

Find your plimsoll line

There is a marker on a ship called a 'plimsoll line' that lets you know when a ship is about to sink from overload. Your mind and body send you signals to let you know your wellbeing is low and you're reaching your 'plimsoll line.' Markers include trouble sleeping, getting cranky about small things, comfort eating, irritability, becoming argumentative and lower than usual levels of patience.

Take a moment to think about how you know you've reached your 'plimsoll line.' Share this with someone close to you who is committed to your health and wellbeing. Let them know these behaviours usually mean you're getting overloaded and might need someone to step in, listen and help problem solve to support you staying afloat.

Know your 'plimsoll line' and try responding proactively to it when you've reached it. A word of caution; this can happen quite often when you're an Educator.

Start your day with hope

As you walk into your classroom each morning, there will be reminders of all the 'to dos' to get through (on top of the existing day's teaching agenda). If you're going through a particularly challenging time with a student or class dynamic, you may find yourself entering a negative thought spiral. The defeating thoughts can easily sabotage how you feel and drain your energy before you've even started your day. Practicing optimism and consciously choosing to have a hopeful outlook for the day ahead can recharge and energise you with what you need to not only survive your day but enjoy it. It takes as much energy to focus your mind on everything you're worried about as it does to focus your mind on all the things that might go right.

Try instilling a habit of greeting your colleagues and students each morning with a hopeful outlook. The flow on effect of optimism can start with you. Saying warm and friendly things like 'What a beautiful day' and 'We're going to leave this classroom today stronger, smarter and better than when we came in' are all ways to wire your thinking with hope. Practicing a hopeful outlook consistently can rewire your brain to feel happier and interpret life in a more positive way. When you're in of a state of contentedness, you're more likely to manage your feelings constructively (Achor 2010).

You can also start your day with hope by revisiting hopeful memories of your work as an Educator.

> When was a time when you had an exceptional teaching breakthrough?
> Who are the students you reached who felt 'unreachable' at the beginning?

When did you surprise yourself with an obstacle you overcame?
What are some of the compliments you've had from students, parents and other Educators?

Drawing upon past experiences of hope and optimism can lift you throughout a difficult time and build stronger networks for hope in your brain (Snyder et al. 2002).

To end your day with hope (which will help you start the next one accordingly), consider creating a daily optimism ritual before you leave your teaching environment. Try and imagine all the good things that might happen the next day, or think of something you're looking forward to. Perhaps make a wish or hope that tomorrow will exceed all expectations and be a great progression from today. Whatever you do, see that good things are coming. Know that the fruits of your effort will grow, even if they seem small or distant right now.

Gratitude

We've all heard it, we all know it's good for us, but why is it so hard to incorporate gratitude into our day? Some people say it seems too simple to be effective. Others report it's hard to remember. The act of noticing what's going well is essential for your wellbeing. Your mind finds it joyful and relaxing to reflect on goodness. Plans will go wrong from one day to the next, usually minor, occasionally major. To keep the 'colour of Educator life' in balance, it's important to recall and savour whatever is going well. After a while the brain builds pathways for noticing the better parts of your day and you naturally start focusing on positive and useful memories rather than negative, unhelpful ones. As a result, your wellbeing lifts.

Many Educators find keeping a gratitude journal on their classroom desk to write in before leaving for the day helps build the practice into their routine. Others prefer to do it as a whole class activity (which is ideal) and others prefer to do it at home. However you choose to practice it, try and create a daily routine at the same time to help you remember.

The following questions can help increase your sense of gratitude. While the first question is ample, for those seeking a deeper experience of gratitude journaling, more questions follow.

1. Name three things that went well today.
2. Why do you think these things went well today?
3. Who are three people you were glad to see today?
4. What is one thing you can see in front of you right now that you're grateful for?
5. What is one thing you're looking forward to tomorrow?

After a few weeks of dedicated writing in a journal, you'll find your mind quite naturally focusing on what's going well.

Positive words jar

The words and communication style you choose are important. Positive words bring about positive feelings. When you draw your attention to it, you'll see negative words bring about negative feelings. It's simple.

Consider an 'audit' on your language and communication style, especially when you're at work or talking about work.

> Start by creating a list of positive words.
> Write them down and place them in a jar.

You can do this as a staff and as a class, allowing everyone to contribute through a brainstorm of positive words.

> At the start of each day, take a word out and display it.
> Reflect on your word as often as you remember throughout the day.
> Do your best to bring that word to life in your thoughts, words and actions.

Speaking in a positive way is mentally energising and harmonising.

Exchanging 'have to' for 'get to'

A day in Education involves teaching, connecting, laughing, conversing and many things you love. There are also the tasks you *have* to do, like lesson preparation, problem solving, follow up, reporting and more. If each day was entirely straightforward, you may potentially feel less content, as there would be fewer opportunities to appreciate the emotional contrast between things going smoothly and the unavoidable bumps in the road.

Perhaps in some ways, it's the colourful blend of uncertainty, obligations and challenges combined with breakthroughs, wins and moments of connectedness that help us feel more grateful in our work as Educators.

When thoughts like '*I have to*' flood your mind about your role, you're likely to experience frustration not only with what needs doing but with how you feel about your job in general. When your mind is dominated by 'I *have to* do this and I *have to* do that,' you can enter a state of pessimism and resistance. Struggling against the inevitable is exhausting and makes everything harder to push through. Remember, the nature of your thoughts will affect the nature of your feelings.

One way to breathe optimism into daily tasks is by saying '*I get to*' when you would otherwise say '*I have to.*' For example, instead of, 'I *have* to finish reports today,' you might say, 'I *get* to finish reports today' (because report writing is a chance to reflect on how much effort you have put in to each student and how far they have come because of your dedication). Instead of 'I *have* to go to work,' think 'I *get* to go to work' (because I have a job where my unique skills and talents are needed and continue having a ripple effect in the years to come).

Next time you hear the words '*have to*' creeping in, try and interrupt them with '*get to.*'

Focus on nature and what's steady in your life

During the Global Pandemic, everything about Education changed on every layer possible. Educators, who are quite used to change and the need to be flexible and adaptable, were naturally and particularly thrown by the pandemic spin. When your entire work environment changes (and keeps changing), it's hard to feel emotionally calm and steady. Being an Educator is a large part of your life. When things are challenging there, it has a flow on effect into all areas of your life.

When life isn't feeling steady, it can help to look for things that are. During the Global Pandemic, the world of Education was up in the air and chaotic. The one constant on school grounds, other than Educator dedication and determination, was nature. Most of the time, except in natural disasters, nature provides a steady place to rest and reset. Making time to observe, appreciate and reflect on it contributes to healthy wellbeing.

There are many hidden treasures in your day that remain unaffected by challenges. Consciously reflecting on these can be very reassuring: your values, the view from your window, that warm cup of coffee . . . all simple things that stay the same despite challenges and changes.

Remember nature and other steady points as anchors that support your wellbeing when external change and disruption are tumbling around you. Indulge in them daily; savour and enjoy them. These simple joys recharge your emotional batteries when you give them the time and conscious attention they deserve.

Email someone every day to thank them

No one succeeds entirely in isolation. It's the warm interconnectedness of a caring community that lifts everyone. We all know how good it feels to be thanked. What you might not know is *you* also benefit from expressing thanks. Taking time to thank others increases your feelings of connection, positivity and gratitude. One way you can do this is by creating a habit of starting or ending your day with a message of thanks to your students or colleagues. It doesn't have to be long and you don't need to look for anything extraordinary.

Thanking students for working hard and trying their best, or simply for being themselves, will not only have an impact on them, it will recharge your energy and enthusiasm, too. Thanking colleagues for being good listeners and Educators for inspiring you, being great people to work with and for always smiling are simple offerings that benefit everyone involved. A school community that thanks each other can help make up for how thankless work in Education can sometimes feel.

After 21 days of writing notes of thanks, optimism and social connection increases significantly (Achor, 2018).

Letting go of control

Being resistant to challenges and trying to control things that are out of your hands can be emotionally draining. The words and actions of others are not yours to manage or control. You can do everything possible to lead your students and school community with compassion and integrity, but it's up to the individual and their circumstances to respond accordingly.

If you hold standards for your students or others that they will behave with the same integrity as you, you're setting yourself up for stress and disappointment. Resistance and frustration are tiring emotions to carry. To maintain optimism and an accepting mindset, you need to acknowledge what you can and can't control. Accept your students and others are doing the best they can with the skills and knowledge they have at the time. Then consciously let it go.

Finding humour in difficult situations

A simple recharge that keep things light during difficulty is looking for a funny side. It's easy to get caught up in knee-jerk feelings and reactions from a colourful day with a challenging classroom dynamic. Sometimes anger and frustration are great messengers and help you think more deeply about what matters to you. At other times, high emotion can mean low intelligence, so it can stop you from thinking clearly, fuel negativity and hold you stuck in the moment.

Some situations when you work in Education are so absurd, you have to laugh. You couldn't conjure it up if you tried. Sometimes (as long as you are being respectful), it's important to stop giving something the level of seriousness you have done previously and enjoy a quiet laugh.

Maintaining humour is essential as an Educator and is an effective alternative for getting stuck in negativity. Unrealistic expectations that your plans should consistently carry out as hoped for can make you feel upset and strengthen your brain's neural pathways for pessimism and helplessness.

If a situation is not one you can laugh about, see if there are other ways to bring more laughter into your day. Watch funny movies and programmes, read funny books, talk to friends with a great sense of humour and actively seek out situations that bring you joy.

Keep things in perspective; bad times aren't forever

When you're struggling with a difficult situation, it can be hard to imagine how you'll survive. The discomfort hurts so much, it feels like it will last forever. Pain is like that. You are now close to, or well and truly at the end of, a Global Pandemic. The excruciating changes and demands felt impossible at the beginning, yet here you are. It passed and you made it.

As an Educator, some days feel like the weight of the world on your shoulders. You know how much potential there is to make a difference, but that also comes with pressure. There are students you work achingly hard to connect with and lead well, but you simply don't see any outcomes to help keep you motivated and hopeful. Sometimes tricky days turn into tricky weeks and beyond. The strain is relentless. There's nothing unusual about feeling like you've been through the ringer at these times. Resilience isn't static. It ebbs and flows. You can't expect to be instantly capable and resilient of handling anything, no matter what.

> Here are some steps you can take to help keep things in perspective and, remember, bad times aren't forever.
>
> 1. Acknowledge the frustration you're feeling. Don't fight it. Allow it to be there.
> 2. Accept there will be periods of difficulty in Education and there's no magic wand to hurry it along.
> 3. Give things time. Your ability to cope will improve as you adjust to your circumstances. You can't hurry challenges, life or progress with a student or class; everything worth doing takes time.
> 4. Do something helpful with your feelings like talking to others, getting outdoors when you have some non-contact time, exercising (even if that involves creating movement breaks where your students are involved), having fun, being creative and choosing to do positive and helpful things.

People have the most incredible ability to adapt and cope with whatever life throws at them. If you're going through a stressful time as an Educator, remember, you're not alone and it's not forever.

Smile

Your brain releases chemicals when you smile that make you feel happier and improve your wellbeing. Creating an artificial smile can trick your mind into feeling happier than you did before you smiled. In one study, researchers found that one smile can make you feel as good as 2,000 bars of chocolate or 16,000 pounds sterling! The same researchers found that smiling also lowers stress, makes your immune system stronger and releases endorphins (your 'feel good' hormones). These feelings of wellbeing are not only for you when you smile, as you pass on good feelings to others.

> Challenge yourself to smile at every student as they enter your class each day. Try to smile at colleagues as much as you can.
> Smile spontaneously for no reason in particular.

Smiling is contagious.

Talk to other Educators

One of the mentally healthiest things I saw emerge from the Global Pandemic was the deep and supportive conversation that opened and the incredible solidarity amongst Educators that followed. Together they were openly united, perhaps more than ever before, about how to move through such an enormous and unprecedented challenge. They already knew their work required tireless dedication, they already felt overwhelmed and exhausted a lot of the time, but they weren't talking about it anywhere near often enough. With the pandemic, an open, global dialogue was launched. Educators started talking openly about their struggles. A full spectrum of emotions was expressed and permission was finally granted within many Educator group cultures to respect and accept it is not possible to have it all together, all the time. Educators started talking to each other about how hard the situation was. Guards went down as everyone was going through the exact same thing at the exact same time. Educators started feeling more comfortable to express their feelings without worrying about being seen as weak or incapable. They were opening up about their feelings with each other. Parents were seeing first-hand how hard it was to educate young people, and they were talking to Educators and checking in on their wellbeing.

Talking about your feelings can never be underestimated. Finding someone trustworthy and reliable who will listen without judgement, journaling privately or talking to a therapist or online/phone counsellor is crucial when you're an Educator. Your students need you to be okay. You need you to be okay.

Let's take this lesson from the Global Pandemic and keep the dialogue between Educators open and, when necessary, raw and vulnerable. Let's allow struggle and not see it as failure. Let's share what we find hard and support and inspire each other through it.

> How can you find time every day to talk about your day? Who would you talk to?

Peer support and mutual mentoring

Think about how recharged you feel after talking things through with another person. Supporting yourself and your colleagues in Education is a great way to improve workplace relationships, learn from each other, problem solve and check in on each other's goals.

> Consider creating pairs or trios each school term amongst your staff to share challenges, victories and goals.
> Each week for a few minutes at staff meeting, people can go into their pair or group to discuss their goals, wins and challenges.
> Each term you can start a new pair or trio, or you might like to keep connected for half a year at a time.

These conversations deepen social connection and compassion in your Educator community, improving the state of wellbeing that comes from healthy relationships in your environment. Peer support, coaching and mentoring is an excellent tool for strengthening connection in your workplace.

Recharge with a digital detox

Mobile phones started out as a way to stay connected and be contactable when we were away from our homes and offices. They are now the centre of many people's lives; naturally intriguing, lovely to hold, easy to navigate and highly addictive. The temptation to quickly scroll social media, check an email or text, send a friend a note or check out an online sale is constant and the perfect distraction when we're feeling uncomfortable or bored. There is also a notorious fear of missing out. As social beings, now connected more than ever before through our devices, we can worry about missing something important if we don't check them often enough.

We have enough evidence to show that most adults are spending too long on device screens. The impact is significant and one that whole books have now been dedicated to. If you feel you could do with a digital detox, here are a handful of questions to get you started:

1   What am I giving up in my personal life to be on my device?
2   What could I do instead of being on screens that I usually don't feel I have time for?
3   Where can I put my devices so they are inconvenient to grab hold of when I'm looking for a 'quick fix' distraction?
4   How many hours am I willing to give up of my week to being on a screen?
5   How can I set limits (as the custodian of how I choose to use my time) so my digital life is not coming at a sacrifice to my real life?
6   What can I follow that makes the social media feed more energising?
7   What can I unfollow that is causing me discomfort?
8   What goals and plans to reach those goals do I have to protect myself against device addiction?

This is not about stopping screen time altogether (and if you tried, you will probably struggle to maintain it long term). This is about bringing your screen use to your awareness, and conducting an audit to consider what you might be giving up in the vacuum that devices can pull you into. Screen time will always have a place in today's digitally connected world; just try not to give screens more place than they deserve.

Change the channel in your mind

There can be a lot to keep up with as an Educator. While you're completely capable of coping and the difficulties are softened by the wins, the wave of negativity that comes from destructive and hopeless thoughts can be strong and repetitive. It can be hard to stop. Try thinking of your mind as a series of channels. There are the angry, negative, hopeless channels along with the happy, positive, hopeful ones. There's also everything in between. Thoughts can be really automatic and hard to train. One way you can try to move on from one 'channel' is to create the habit of asking yourself to simply 'change the channel.' This is a quick and easy way to shift your mind onto something else. Simply imagine you have a remote control in your hand and you flick the channel when you've had enough and need a recharge.

Create an abundant mindset by thinking about what *is* good, what *has* gone well and how far you *have* come

Hardworking Educators may find themselves at the end of the day mulling over the challenges they experienced, the strategies that didn't go according to plan and the massive to-do list that lies ahead of them for the next day. This is not because they are the type to moan or because they have a negative outlook. It comes from their dedication to the future of young people. If something didn't go well or work, they want to know why and get to the bottom of it so they can make it better and help their students thrive.

Ending your working day with a deficit mindset is taxing and can have a negative impact on your mental wellbeing. Feeling like you're not enough and that the outlook ahead is somewhat hopeless won't allow you to recharge your wellbeing battery.

Try and recharge your mind with hope every day. Look at what *is* going well in your role in Education. Pay attention to what you *do* have to support your work as an Educator. Remember how far you *have* come over the years. Educators work isn't straightforward or easy – so it will always experience bumps in the road. Remind yourself that you've already proven time and again that you're capable of rising to this level of complexity. There are many fruits of your labour around you. Allow time to see, celebrate and be energised by them.

Take a piece of paper or journal and answer the following questions:

1. Name five or more things that are going well in your work as an Educator.
2. Name five or more things you already have to support your role as an Educator that you're grateful for.
3. Name five achievements you're proud of to recognise how far you've already come in your role as an Educator.

In your daily practice, you don't need to come up with five examples for each area (unless you want to). Taking the time to build an abundant mindset by acknowledging the good in your work and recognising how far you've come as an Educator will help you recharge from your day without a looming sense of not having done enough.

Compassion for yourself and others

Compassion means empathically putting yourself in another person's shoes and showing that awareness through gestures of acceptance, understanding and support. Compassion helps you see the best in others, as you look far beyond the surface of how someone presents to you.

A compassionate mindset is crucial in Education. Looking out for yourself and others through understanding and acceptance helps strengthen the social thread of a school community. Schools can be emotionally charged places. Children co-exist, all at different stages of development, with their social–emotional 'learner's plates' on. Conflict, misunderstanding and emotional dysregulation are bound to happen between them. Without compassion for yourself as an Educator being faced with this every day, along with compassion for your students, who are still learning and will naturally struggle, your wellbeing will suffer. Compassion for your colleagues, who are also experiencing a diverse range of experiences, will help tame your frustrations when you see something in them that's different to your values, capabilities and style as an Educator.

There's an added bonus to compassion too. Being compassionate brings about comfortable and energising feelings that support your wellbeing. Giving and receiving compassion reduces loneliness, conflict and feelings of social disconnection. Studies have consistently shown the brain reacts most positively when you're kind and compassionate (Cooper, Krerps, Wiebe, Pirkl and Knutson, 2010). Compassion also helps you feel less reactive to different personalities and can prevent knee-jerk reactions, negative judgements and aggressive communication.

A compassionate Educator trains themselves to stay calm, stop or reduce judgemental mind chatter and respond with empathy and understanding – or at the very least by remaining neutral. A compassionate Educator understands you can never fully know all the reasons why a child or colleague comes across the way they do. A compassionate Educator runs off the assumption that everyone is doing the best they can with the skills, knowledge, character and experience they have at the time. It's not by any means easy to consistently think this way. It takes steady effort and personal reminders.

Self-compassion is compassion reversed back onto yourself. You know the drill – put your oxygen mask on first before helping others. This one can be tough for many Educators. Often confronted throughout the day with their student's needs which are often immediate and demanding, Educators may find themselves providing exceptional care for their students and their families, while in the process unintentionally allowing their own wellbeing to be compromised.

When you show yourself compassion, you respect your personal boundaries and needs to take a break, rest, play, exercise and lead a whole and fulfilling life. You allow yourself to be imperfect, a maker of mistakes and regrets, a person who still has so much to learn. Investing in self-compassion doesn't come naturally to most, nor does compassion, so take time to build these skills and be patient with your progress.

When you can feel unconditional acceptance and understanding for yourself and others, you can emotionally recharge easier from the mishaps you will inevitably encounter each day.

Moving forward, think about how to make self-compassion a priority when the world is still catching up with making wellbeing a priority. If you wait for it to be policy or valued in every workplace, you might be waiting a while and your wellbeing will continue to suffer. Everyone can take their wellbeing into their own hands, be responsible for it and start as small as necessary, perhaps through the act of self-compassion.

Here are some ways you can show yourself self-compassion:

1. *Let yourself be imperfect.* Accept and forgive your mistakes. There are many variables in a school community and what might work one day may not on another. To know what to do with every student, every single time, is impossible. No matter how much you've studied and pondered about Education, your work can't be simplified into one approach or a handful of simple solutions. Students, class dynamics and the emotional climate are not static. You have to be flexible, adaptable and quick thinking throughout the day.
2. *Avoid comparing yourself to other Educators.* How you teach, support and respond will be different from how others teach, support and respond. When these differences are admirable to you, they can serve as inspiration, not as evidence that they are doing a better job than you.
3. *Take time to rest from your Educator role.* Even when there's a student you're worried about or a new challenge you're resolving, these should not come ahead of your rest at the end of the day. Try and stick to a time each night where your work ends and rest begins. Avoid checking email until the next day.
4. *Respect yourself and expect others to respect you too.* Your students *and* you come first. You're *both* a priority. Neither should suffer at the hands of the other. You're allowed to have boundaries and you're entitled to receive care and respect.

Developing self-compassion and compassion take time, practice and patience. Be patient with yourself in the process.

Rest

While there is a whole chapter about resting and recovery, it's important to recognise that rest is crucial for recharging your batteries. Taking time to rest and getting enough sleep each night is an important daily recharge. If you struggle with sleep it's important to seek support, as the quality of your sleep will have a ripple effect across your day. Educators need daily rest to have enough mental and physical energy to cope with the nature of their work.

References

Achor, S. (2010). *The Happiness Advantage: The Seven Principles of Positive Psychology That Fuel Success and Performance at Work*. New York: Currency.

Achor, S. (2018). *Big Potential: How Transforming the Pursuit of Success Raises Our Achievement, Happiness, and Wellbeing*. New York: Currency.

Cooper, J. C., Krerps, T. A., Wiebe, T., Pirkl, T. and Knutson, B. (2010). When Giving Is Good: Ventromedial Prefrontal Cortex Activation for Others' Intentions. *Neuron*, 67 (3), 511–521. DOI:10.1016/j.neuron.2010.06030.

Snyder, C., Shorey, H., Cheavans, J., Pulvers, K., Ill, V. and Wiklund, C. (2002). Hope and Academic Success in College. *Journal of Educational Psychology*, 94, 820–826. DOI:10.1037/0022-0663.94.4.820.

4 A license to rest and recover

How often do we engage in rest and recovery without feeling selfish or indulgent? Consider all the daily roles Educators carry as they work towards student progress and outcomes. Each needs time to rest and recover from. Some professions embraced some rest during the 2020 Global Pandemic. Like many other frontline and essential workers (including parents), this license was not available to Educators. Without daily rest, especially when life throws a curveball, a backlog of exhaustion is inevitable.

Developing simple daily rituals for rest and recovery is important in any job and Educators are no exception. The strategies in this chapter will help you find tools to rest and recover mentally, physically and emotionally.

Breathing

While it might be tempting to skip this strategy, there's a reason it has first place in the chapter. Diaphragmatic breathing has been empirically proven to improve attention, lower stress and increase physical and mental health (Xiao Ma et al. 2017). Breathing in oxygen and breathing out carbon dioxide through diaphragmatic breathing lowers blood pressure and slows your heartbeat, calming the nerves (Zaccaro et al. 2018). Regulated breathing techniques enhance wellbeing, providing you with a skill you can control and access at any time. It reduces stress, improves sleep and increases your physical health (Oguz et al. 2019).

Educators support the social, emotional and academic growth of young people. They carry the responsibility that their work matters a great deal with the potential to be a life changing force in all their student's lives. This is an enormous privilege and weight to carry. Without daily rest and conscious rituals like diaphragmatic breathing, Educator wellbeing will suffer.

There are many different ways to learn to control your breath. Find the ways that suit you best and build a toolbox of breathing techniques. Try not to overlook breathing because it's so simple and accessible. The evidence demonstrates it is a highly effective way to calm difficult feelings, relax and return to mental clarity. As you slow your breath, you slow your mind.

Diaphragmatic breathing and progressive muscle relaxation sequence

When emotions become charged, your fight–flight–freeze reaction can dysregulate your breathing and increase your muscle tension. The direct relationship between muscle tension and your sympathetic and parasympathetic nervous systems mean that when your muscles are tight and tense, your nervous system follows suit. When your muscles are soft and relaxed, you nerves are more settled, too.

During progressive muscle relaxation, focus on different muscle groups in a specific order, tensing and relaxing each for several seconds and taking deep breaths between muscle groups (McCallie, Blum and Hood 2006).

Each time you hold a muscle tight aim for 10 seconds of tension and 20 seconds of muscle release time. Allow a moment between each muscle group to take three slow and deep breaths.

> Lie on the floor and close your eyes. Notice how your body is feeling. Is it tense? Is it relaxed? Is it somewhere in between?
> Take in three slow, deep breaths through your nose and out through tight-pursed lips.
> Start with your face . . .
> Lift your eyebrows up as high as you can. Hold . . . and release.
> Take three slow, deep breaths.
> Smile widely like a clown in a sideshow alley. Hold . . . and release.
> Take three slow, deep breaths.
> Lift your shoulders up high like you're trying to touch your ears. Hold . . . and release.
> Take three slow, deep breaths.
> Tense your arms straight and tight, making a fist at the end. Hold . . . and release.
> Take three slow, deep breaths.
> Press your hands into the ground with your arms back against the floor like you're trying to push them into the floor away from you. Hold . . . and release.
> Take three slow, deep breaths.
> Squeeze your bottom as tight as you can. Hold . . . and release.
> Take three slow, deep breaths.
> Tighten your thigh muscles. Hold . . . and release.
> Take three slow, deep breaths.
> Pull your feet towards you so your feet and calf muscles grow tight. Hold . . . and release.
> Take three slow, deep breaths.
> Lift your arms up over your head and point your toes downward making yourself as tall as you can. Hold . . . and release.
> Take three slow, deep breaths.

Repeat the sequence up to three more times and pay attention to how your body feels at the end compared to the start. A great way to end progressive muscle relaxation is with a guided meditation or visualisation.

Breathing meditation

This can be a great way to start and end your day.

- Close your eyes and notice the sounds around you.
- Place one hand on your stomach and the other on your chest.
- Quietly focus on your breath going in and out, making your stomach rise.
- See if you can slow your breathing down a little.
- In your own time, breathe in and out, in and out.
- Keep noticing your breath. Every time you start thinking about something else re-focus on your breathing. In and out . . . in and out.
- Enjoy the quiet for a while. You don't need to think about anything but your breathing.

Sleeping better through conscious breathing

Many Educators struggle to gain a good night's sleep, going over the day that's been and looking ahead to the day ahead. Focusing on your breath can help you fall asleep at night, especially if you tend to stay up worrying or thinking things through. When you can't fall asleep, one strategy is to bring your mind back to your breath. In your mind, track each breath you take (breathing in, breathing out and continue). Every time a thought enters, go back to thinking about your breath until you fall back asleep. There are many other strategies that help with sleep like meditation, playing gentle or white noise, reducing time on devices, following a regular bed time routine, taking an evening walk, reading a book to wind down and so on.

Mindfulness and presence

Being present and mindful are important ways to keep things in perspective and support your wellbeing. A lot of worry and stress comes from reliving past obstacles and worrying about future challenges. Students that need extra support can sometimes unintentionally keep you in a state of high alert, making it hard to be present and mindful when they are in front of you. Once you get the hang of staying present and in the moment with them, you might see some unexpected benefits. You may find it easier to relate to them when you meet them exactly where they are, instead of where you want them to be or worry that they won't be. You will also feel calmer and more regulated, despite whatever is happening in front of you.

The practice of mindfulness (being completely and non-judgementally engaged in what you are doing right now) is not (in its traditional form) for everyone and certainly isn't easy. You might not be able to slow down and be present on command, but perhaps there are other ways you can enter this state, like when you're doing something you love, soaking up a beautiful view or while reading a book. Try not to feel restricted by the traditional definitions and, instead, take on the meaning and find how that fits in with your life.

Mindfulness has many benefits including reduced stress and rumination and better emotional regulation (Gu, Strauss, Bond and Cavanagh (2015)). Staying in a mindful state takes conscious effort and most people will tell you that just moments after planning to stay in the present, their mind starts wandering. By nature, our minds unconsciously chatter. We become so used to hearing those thoughts, we might not even notice it's happening.

Overactive and unregulated negative thoughts about the past and future are powerful, influencing your state of mind. To be present and mindful, you need to acknowledge the thoughts that bombard your mind, then let them go, returning your attention to what is presently in front of you. If you're with another person and you're fully present with them, your connection can expand. Your presence without distraction makes people feel seen, heard and understood. A distracted companion, on the other hand, makes others feel rushed, dismissed and disconnected.

The flood of information through devices, email, messengers and social media are constant reminders that even if you're still for a moment, the rest of the world isn't. Most people are fighting the urge to step out of the present to find out what's happening around them. The impulse to sneak a look at your device can be hard to resist, constantly interrupting your presence. Mindfulness and presence are a necessity in a fast-paced, changing world.

Learning to be mindful encourages the brain into an 'approach' state where you are comfortable about facing and dealing with your challenges rather than avoiding them, wiring your brain for resilience (Siegel 2010).

Our minds are naturally busy and mindfulness is more attainable on some days but not others. Try not to be hard on yourself as you master this skill. If you're searching for a deeper understanding of mindfulness and more tools, you might like to look into a book dedicated solely to the topic.

Giving the moment in front of you your full and undivided attention

Another way of looking at presence and mindfulness is by simply doing whatever you are doing with your full attention. Committing completely to the moment in front of you, the only moment that is there for certain, builds your mindfulness muscles.

Next time you're driving, perhaps, see if you can practice this. (We should be doing this anyway, but everyone knows that when you're driving, it's so automatic that your mind will often drift to the day ahead, or the one that's past or something else.) As you drive, make a commitment to completely attend to what you presently hear, see and feel. Think about where you are that moment and what is in front of you. You can try this again when you're at the grocery store or while eating a meal. The more you can practice committing fully to the moment in front of you, the easier mindfulness becomes.

Pause for presence breaks

A short daily break where classes pause to be present can help your school community transition into a calm state of awareness, soothing your minds and recharging your batteries. Just like the play and lunch bell, what if there were a bell to remind everyone to pause for three minutes? Through regular pausing practice, neural pathways are strengthened, helping you to intuitively focus on the present when thoughts and feelings threaten to overwhelm you.

- Begin your 'pause for presence' breaks with something to indicate a change in atmosphere, like a music bell, turning the lights off in the classroom, playing soothing music or tapping on a gong.
- Everyone closes their eyes. Lead everyone to breathe in and out at their own pace. As you breathe in, count 1 . . . 2 . . . 3 and as you breathe out, count 1 . . . 2 . . . 3. The conscious breathing is done in your mind, not out loud.
- Once everyone is in a solid breathing rhythm, notice what can you hear. What can you smell? What can you feel? What can you feel?

This is a simple way to instill the value of slowing down and resetting that doesn't take up much time and benefits everyone's wellbeing.

Mindful walking

A simple way to practice mindfulness and train yourself to be present is by taking a mindful walk. As you walk, aim to focus on nothing more than the sensation of walking and what your senses notice as you move along.

Your mind will potentially bombard you with other thoughts unrelated to your walk. Acknowledge their presence and try to return your mind to walking. You can add mindful walking whenever you are walking from your classroom to your car each afternoon. Mindful walking needs to be reserved for a time when you're unlikely to be interrupted (so usually when there are no students left on the grounds – or during your free time).

Mindful eating and drinking

Another easy method to build your mindfulness muscles is to eat your food more consciously. Often, it's easier to grab a meal and quickly scoff it down, barely noticing its rich textures and flavours.

> Choose something simple like an apple or a cup of tea.
> Can you keep your mind focused on the process and sensation of eating or drinking?
> As thoughts enter, acknowledge them. Then return your mind to the taste, texture and smell of what you're eating or drinking.

You might like to practice this on your lunch break or after your class leaves for the day to wholly experience the pleasure of eating something.

Another way to make it part of your week is to do it with your class. Here's an example of what you might do if you practiced it as a whole class:

> Provide everyone with something like a raisin or piece of dark chocolate.
> Lead the group to look at the food, consciously observing its appearance.
> Direct everyone's attention towards smelling it and savouring the scent.
> Next, focus on touching it. What does it feel like in your hand or on your fingertips? Pay attention to the details.
> Finally, students can place it in their mouth, noticing every bite, enjoying the flavour and feeling until it's gone.
>
> (Parker 2020)

Mindful breathing: the 4–7–8 method

While there are many effective breathing techniques, it's important to try a few and find the ones that suit you. Some find tracking their breath consciously is effective enough for calming and clearing their mind. Tracking your breath is being conscious of each breath in your mind, narrating what your breath is doing (I'm breathing in and out, in an out, in and out . . .).

How to 4–7–8:

> Breathe in slowly to the count of four seconds.
> Hold your breath for seven seconds.
> Breathe out slowly (through tight, pursed lips) for eight seconds.
> Take a few regular slow breaths in between and repeat 4–7–8 at least five times.
>
> (Weil 1998)

Play music you love

There are many known scientific benefits to listening to music, including its contribution to pain-relief and improving your mood (Onevia 2013). Listening to uplifting music creates changes in your brain's pleasure centres, as well as releasing the feel-good hormone dopamine. Increases in dopamine have even been noted in people who are thinking about music. Instrumental musicthat is shown to make you feel happy is referred to by researchers at the Montreal Neurological Institute as 'chill' songs. They are songs that gave the listeners 'chills,' causing the brain to release dopamine. They include 'Claire de Lune' by Debussy; 'First Breath After Coma' by Explosions in the Sky; and 'Adagio for Strings' (Parade of the Athletes Version) by Tiesto (Salimpoor, Beovoy and Zatorre 2011).

Playing uplifting background music supports a positive mood, contributing to emotional wellbeing.

A study using the *Australian Unity Wellbeing Index* identified six areas of music consumption to improve wellbeing; listening to music, dancing, singing, playing an instrument, attending concerts and composing music. People engaging in high levels of music consumption rated vastly better on levels of happiness and wellbeing. Within this group, the leading scores were from those regularly attending concerts and going out dancing. This result was linked to the social connection both activities tended to bring with them (Weinberg and Joseph 2017). Finding ways to increase music consumption can help improve your own and your students' wellbeing.

Playing music in your classroom and even in the school yard during play and meal breaks are some ways to bring more music into the environment. In one school I visit, the traditional school bell has been exchanged for upbeat Top 40 music. Every time the bell goes, I feel a pang of joy – and even though the students are disappointed to see their play period come to a halt, I see joy in their faces as they sing or hum along to a song on their way to return to class.

Watch what you watch

With the news at your fingertips through mobile technology and social media, it's hard not to know when something goes wrong in the world. Negative news was the only news for a very long time during the Global Pandemic, enough to crush hope and wellbeing.

Watching just three minutes of negative news in the morning was found to increase a person's likelihood of reporting an unhappy day six hours later by 27 percent (Achor and Gielan 2015). Watching negative images such as those in violent video games have shown an increase in aggression and a decrease in empathy and prosocial behaviour (Anderson et al. 2010).

Educators often tell me that by the time they get home from a long day, all they feel like doing is watching television or binging on social media. With both will come news flashes that bring unhappiness right into your home. What you watch really does matter and it's important to find the courage to turn it off, or at the very least reduce how much you watch, even though it's drawing you in and begging you to do otherwise.

Do something for fun, without a goal or purpose

Do you engage in activities just for the fun of it? Even pleasurable activities like hobbies and pastimes are often done with a purpose in mind. Take, for example, a hike. You might love hiking and engage in it often. It's likely you see the hike as a form of exercise, too, and this becomes a core reason you keep doing it. Without a purpose or reason, people often think what they are doing is indulgent or unnecessary. Fun for the sake of fun is valuable to your wellbeing.

It's important to remember you don't have to be 'good' at something to delve in and enjoy it either. Many people avoid creative endeavours that could bring about a lot of fun because they don't see themselves as good enough.

Creative pursuits like painting, writing, poetry, sewing, crafting and gardening allow you to be present, mindful and enter a state of flow. Try avoiding the expectation that you'll be an expert immediately. Go in for the fun of it and see what happens. Mastery takes time.

Journaling: fun for the sake of fun

Write a list of activities that interest you. Set a challenge to have a go at something new and creative.

Consciously focus on nature

Whether it's having pictures in your classroom and staff room that depict nature, or gazing your eyes towards windows, nature can help bring you to a more restful emotional state. In one study, people who looked at photographs with the most green and blue from nature showed lower frustration, greater levels of calm and better engagement (Aspinall et al. 2015).

Take a look at your environment, the colours and style of decorations.

> Is there a way to bring more harmonising colours like green and blue into your space? Would an indoor plant or a bunch of fresh foliage contribute to the feeling in the room?
> Can you get your students involved too so they enjoy the benefits of being part of the uplifting mood you're creating?

Make time for inactivity

Trying to be productive all the time can be nothing short of exhausting. It's important to bring inactivity into your day so you can catch your breath and recover. Moments of inactivity are rare in most people's lives and Educators are well known for their dedication and hefty work load long after the students have left their classroom.

Consider making a daily 'appointment' for a moment of inactivity. Award yourself five minutes or more a day to enjoy this unique and rejuvenating feeling. If two minutes is all you can find for now, it's a start. Think carefully about when you could add this into your day. Easy periods include right before bed, straight after dinner, before getting out of your car and arriving home and when you have some non-contact time in your classroom. Try and think of a time, book it like an appointment, and see how it makes you feel.

Rest

To recover from anything, you've got to have rest. Yet rest makes many people feel guilty. Others feel uncomfortable about resting, because as long as they are busy they don't have to face what's going on in their mind.

Finding time to rest is crucial in a job where there are few breaks and an inevitable, ongoing mental load. There are many ways to rest. Start by writing down all the things you engage in that you find restful, and see if you can include at least one of these every day. If you genuinely can't do this every day, it's crucial you rest every weekend, then 'lean into' taking rest by adding one weekday at a time until every day of the week has a rest period.

Rest can be anything from reading a book, taking a relaxed walk, sitting in your garden, listening to an audio book in bed, lying down and so forth.

Find out what brings you a state of restfulness and regularly include it in your life.

Creativity

You don't have to be traditionally 'good' at being creative to enjoy it and find it relaxing. Most Educators have the strength of creativity already, by nature of their work with young people. A creative project can hit the mark for helping you rest and recover from your day or week. Anything from doodling on a bit of paper to cooking, writing poetry, painting, gardening and rearranging the aesthetic in your home or classroom are all ways to get the creative juices flowing and help you recover from your day.

Meditation

This can be as simple as doing nothing and sitting in the stillness for a few minutes, or it can involve a more detailed method like guided mediation. There are many long-term and immediate benefits to meditation including lower blood pressure, increased blood flow, improved immunity and even pain relief. Meditation promotes alpha waves in your brain, which relax your nervous system.

In short, meditation is focused concentration and awareness on something, whether it be your breath, a mantra, a candle or other object or a pleasant word in your mind. You can try clearing your thoughts, but even experienced meditators will tell you mental chatter is hard to clear – it does keep entering. If you're trying to clear your mind, simply acknowledge the presence of these interruptions and try and focus on your breath and mental silence.

The loving kindness meditation

The following meditation helps build your kindness muscles and takes just ten minutes a day. Research shows that after engaging in this meditation for 21 days, there was an increase in people's ability to turn outward and show care and compassion for others, as well as a reduction in selfishness (Seppala et al. 2014).

This is a good one to do as a whole class or in small groups. You can reduce how much of it you do if time is limited. Someone will need to read it to you, or you can record it on a device to play as needed.

> Close your eyes. Sit comfortably with your feet flat on the floor and your spine straight. Relax your whole body. Keep your eyes closed throughout

the whole visualisation and bring your awareness inward. Without straining or concentrating, just relax and gently follow the instructions. Take a deep breath in. And breathe out.

Receiving loving kindness

Keeping your eyes closed, think of a person close to you who loves you very much. It could be someone from the past or the present; someone still alive or who has passed; it could be a spiritual teacher or guide. Imagine that person standing on your right side sending you their love. That person is sending you wishes for your safety, for your wellbeing and happiness. Feel the warm wishes and love coming from that person towards you.

Now bring to mind the same person or another person who cherishes you deeply. Imagine that person standing on your left side sending you wishes for your wellness, for your health and happiness. Feel the kindness and warmth coming to you from that person.

Now imagine that you are surrounded on all sides by all the people who love you and have loved you. Picture all of your friends and loved ones surrounding you. They are standing sending you wishes for your happiness, wellbeing and health. Bask in the warm wishes and love coming from all sides. You are filled and overflowing with warmth and love.

Sending loving kindness to loved ones

Now bring your awareness back to the person standing on your right side. Begin to send the love that you feel back to that person. You and this person are similar. Just like you, this person wishes to be happy. Send all your love and warm wishes to that person.

Repeat the following phrases, silently:

> May you live with ease, may you be happy, may you be free from pain.
> May you live with ease, may you be happy, may you be free from pain.
> May you live with ease, may you be happy, may you be free from pain.

Now focus your awareness on the person standing on your left side. Begin to direct the love within you to that person. Send all your love and warmth to that person. That person and you are alike. Just like you, that person wishes to have a good life.

Repeat the following phrases, silently:

> Just as I wish to, may you be safe, may you be healthy, may you live with ease and happiness.
> Just as I wish to, may you be safe, may you be healthy, may you live with ease and happiness.

Just as I wish to, may you be safe, may you be healthy, may you live with ease and happiness.

Now picture another person that you love, perhaps a relative or a friend. This person, like you, wishes to have a happy life. Send warm wishes to that person.
Repeat the following phrases, silently:

May your life be filled with happiness, health, and wellbeing.
May your life be filled with happiness, health, and wellbeing.
May your life be filled with happiness, health, and wellbeing.

Sending loving kindness to neutral people

Now think of a colleague in Education, someone you don't know very well and toward whom you do not have any particular feeling. You and this person are alike in your wish to have a good life.
Send all your wishes for wellbeing to that person, repeating the following phrases silently:

Just as I wish to, may you also live with ease and happiness.
Just as I wish to, may you also live with ease and happiness.
Just as I wish to, may you also live with ease and happiness.

Now bring to mind another acquaintance toward whom you feel neutral. It could be a neighbour, or a grocer, or someone else that you see around but do not know very well. Like you, this person wishes to experience joy and wellbeing in his or her life.
Send all your good wishes to that person, repeating the following phrases silently:

May you be happy, may you be healthy, may you be free from all pain.
May you be happy, may you be healthy, may you be free from all pain.
May you be happy, may you be healthy, may you be free from all pain.

Sending loving kindness to all living beings

Now expand your awareness and picture the whole globe in front of you as a little ball.
Send warm wishes to all living beings on the globe who, like you, want to be happy:

Just as I wish to, may you live with ease, happiness and good health.
Just as I wish to, may you live with ease, happiness and good health.
Just as I wish to, may you live with ease, happiness and good health.

Take a deep breath in. And breathe out. And another deep breath in, and let it go. Notice the state of your mind and how you feel after this meditation. When you're ready, you may open your eyes.

Research on the benefits of practicing the loving kindness meditation continue to grow.

Find enjoyable movements to slow challenging feelings from building, so rest and recovery come easier to you

Research has demonstrated the value of daily exercise to improve happiness and wellbeing (Zhang and Chen, 2018). You don't have to join a gym, jog for miles or climb to the top of your closest mountain. Add some form of movement into each day, even if it starts out as getting up every hour and taking a walk around your house, garden or office. The human body is designed to move and serves you best when it is moving often. Moving is often the last thing Educators may want to do after a long day working, learning or engaging in difficult things; yet movement can be your daily reset button that makes all these challenges easier to live with. While moving doesn't feel restful at the time, walking and running for 30 minutes can make a huge difference to your recovery from your day and your preparation for entering a state of rest.

Reading for fun – not for professional development

If you love a good book, are you making enough time to read for the sake of fun, not professional development? For those of you who simply can't find the time during school term, consider gifting yourself a new book at the end of each term to enjoy during the holidays. Reading for yourself and your interests outside of work is important for your wellbeing and can bring you a unique sense of rest and recovery.

Take a moment to write a list of all the books you would like to read, talk to colleagues and friends about what they are reading and let yourself have this luxury if it's meaningful to you. Consider a staff book club where you all get an opportunity to choose a book and share it with anyone who is interested. This can be a great way to connect in a new way and squeeze in some extra reading. You can also have a book club and all be reading your own choices – and simply catch up to talk about what you're reading.

Water

While studies on why water seems to have such a profoundly relaxing effect on people is still in its infancy, most people will agree there is a particularly beautiful sensation that happens when you're around water. Looking at the ocean, sitting by a lake, or watching the rain or a waterfall somehow seem to provide instant relief and relaxation, as if the water is cleansing your mind in its flow.

Here are some simple ways to bring water into your day:

1. Drink water. Keep a water bottle on your desk.
2. Spray on water. Keep a small spray bottle nearby (you might like to add a favourite scent to it) and spray it on your face when you need to recover.
3. Add a small water feature to your classroom through an aquarium, a bowl of water with rocks and other decorations in it or a nice little miniature waterfall decoration.
4. Add artwork or posters that feature water and nature.
5. Make time to take a bath or shower to mentally cleanse at the end of the day, or swim in a pool if you have that luxury.

Create time for 'flow'

Flow is similar to the 'zone' you may hear sports people talk about. It's a state you enter when you are completely absorbed, losing track of time and place in an activity you enjoy. Flow tends to happen most when you're active or creative. Flow supports your wellbeing and resilience.

Creating time for activities that bring you flow will improve your quality of life, happiness, wellbeing and resilience. An important part of flow is engaging in an activity that is challenging at one level above your current abilities, so make sure you step out of your comfort zone to keep the flow effective (Csikszentmihalyi 2008).

'Flow' is a healthy wellbeing state that cannot be rushed into and out of. It can take time after starting an activity to engage in the experience of flow – and sometimes getting started itself is the hardest part (Csikszentmihalyi 2008).

To find your flow, try answering these questions:

- If you could do one thing for fun every day, what would it be?
- Out of all your activities and routines, which one goes by the quickest, leaving you feeling surprised at just how much time has passed?
- Which lessons might you enter a state of flow while teaching?

Once you know what your flow is, talk to a friend, colleague or partner and ask them to help you make time for it to help you rest and recover from your day and week.

Find a wellbeing 'shake off'

Have you ever noticed a duck shake off its feelings after a squabble with another duck? Dogs engage in a similar 'shake off' after interacting with another dog or feeling stressed. Animals are present beings and have built-in mechanisms to move on after a problem.

Animals in conflict tend to move towards each other to 'have it out.' They move about rambunctiously for a while. Soon after, they resolve things – or agree to disagree, heading off in opposite directions. When they are far away enough from the other, they 'shake off' what just happened and calmly move on to the next thing, like nothing ever happened.

Humans, on the other hand, tend to get agitated and stay upset for hours, days and in some cases, years. Without some kind of emotional 'shake off,' painful feelings can linger, becoming harmful and lowering wellbeing.

Try thinking of ways your body 'shakes off' stress. Is it through rest? Movement? Laughter? TV? Find what helps you leave tough moments behind and allows you to rest and recover.

Throughout your day at work, schedule in some 'shake offs' with your students so you all get the benefit of this stress release.

Bring pride to your mind

Help you mind recover each day and enter a restful and harmonious state by thinking of something that brought you feelings of pride. It might be a conversation you had with a colleague or student or perhaps something you handled calmly and respectfully. It might be a personal moment of pride that had nothing to do with anyone else. As you walk out of your classroom each day, enjoy a sense of pride in yourself as an Educator.

Whole school pyjama/comfort wear days

How good does it feel to be in clothes that throw you into a state of restfulness the moment you put them on? Students love a pyjama day and why not get Educators involved too? Not just once a year, but maybe every term, everyone has the license to come to school with cosy clothes or pyjamas on. Learning can continue as usual – or you can dedicate these days to rest and recovery, nurturing wellbeing. If you can't make this work in your school, make sure you give yourself time on the weekends and school holidays to lounge around in comfortable gear, indulging in little more than rest and recovery.

Music, podcasts and radio

Most people enjoy listening to something on their commute to and from work. If you're one of them, allow yourself this treat every day. Consciously choose something that will bring you joyful and restful feelings and make sure you put it on to help move your mind away from the day you've had into a state recovery for the rest period ahead. While it might be tempting to listen to podcasts focusing on Education, try not to do this in isolation and listen to plenty of things that bring you joy for the sake of joy. Try not to bring the pressure of professional development into your rest and recovery time.

If you're working through this book as a staff, break into small groups and share your favourite podcasts/music and radio stations, encouraging each other to step out of your comfort zone and explore some new themes.

Massage

While massage is generally considered a luxury item, it can help you experience deep relaxation that's important for someone in your field of work. If cost is holding you back like most people, consider a massage on your next gift wish list for Christmas or your birthday. Some schools I've worked with have engaged a wellness trainer for staff meetings to learn ways to give yourself and others a short, safe, non-intrusive and gentle massage to make regular massage more accessible. While some people don't like a massage, many appreciate its benefits and the deep feelings of relaxation that follow.

References

Achor, S. and Gielan, M. (2015). Consuming Negative News Can Make You Less Effective at Work. Emotional Intelligence, Harvard Business Review.
Anderson, C. A., Shibuya, A., Ihori, N., Swing, E. L., Bushman, B. J., Sakamoto, A., Rothstein, H. R. and Saleem, M. (2010). Violent Video Game Effects on Aggression, Empathy, and Prosocial Behavior in Eastern and Western Countries: A Meta-Analytic Review. *Psychological Bulletin*, 136 (2), 151–173. https://doi.org/10.1037/a0018251.
Aspinall, P., Mavros, P., Coyne, R., et al. (2015). The Urban Brain: Analysing Outdoor Physical Activity with Mobile EEG. *British Journal of Sports Medicine*, 49, 272–276.
Csikszentmihalyi. (2008).
Gu, J., Strauss, C., Bond, R. and Cavanagh, K. (2015). How Do Mindfulness-Based Cognitive Therapy and Mindfulness-Based Stress Reduction Improve Mental Health and Wellbeing? A Systematic Review and Meta-Analysis of Mediation Studies. *Clinical Psychology Review*, 37C. DOI:10.1016/j.cpr.2015.01.006.
McCallie, M. S., Blum, C. M. and Hood, C. J. (2006). Progressive Muscle Relaxation. *Journal of Human Behavior in the Social Environment*, 13 (3), 51–66. https://doi.org/10.1300/J137v13n03_04.
Nawana Parker, M. (2020). *The Confident Minds Curriculum: Creating a Culture of Personal Growth and Social Awareness*. London: Routeldge.
Onevia-Zafra, M.D., Catro-Sanchez, A. M., Mataran-Pennarorocha, G.A., and Moreno-Lorenzo C. (2013). Effect of Music as Nursing Intervention for People Diagnosed with Fibromyalgia. *Pain Management Nursing 14*, no. 2.
Salimpoor, V., Benovoy, M., Larcher, K. et al. (2011). Anatomically Distinct Dopamine Release during Anticipation and Experience of Peak Emotion to Music. *Nature Neuroscience Journal 14*: 14, 257–262. https://doi.org/10.1038/nn.2726.
Salimpoor V.N., Beevoy, M and Zatorre R (2011). Anatomically Distinct Dopamine Release During Anticipation and Experience of Peak Emotion Music. *Nature Neuroscience Journal* 14: 257–262.
Seppala, E. M., Hutcherson, C. A., Nguyen, D. T. et al. (2014). Loving-Kindness Meditation: A Tool to Improve Healthcare Provider Compassion, Resilience, and Patient Care. *Journal of Compassionate Health Care*, 1, 5. https://doi.org/10.1186/s40639-014-0005-9.
Siegel, D. (2010). The Mindful Therapist: A Clinician's Guide to Mindsight and Neural Integration. *The Humanistic Psychologist*, 38 (3), 244–248. DOI:10.1080/08873267.2010.512253.
Weil, A. (1998). *The 4-7-8 Breath: Health Benefits & Demonstration*. ©2015 Weil Lifestyle. www.drweil.com/drw/u/VDR00112/The-4-7-8-Breath-Benefitsand-Demonstration.html.

Weinberg, M. K. and Joseph, D. (2017). If You're Happy and You Know It: Music Engagement and Subjective Wellbeing. *Psychology of Music 45, no. 2* 45 (2). DOI:10.1177/0305735616659552.

Xiao Ma, Zi-Qi Yue, Zhu-Qing Gong, Hong Zhang, Nai-Yue Duan, Yu-Tong Shi, Gao-Xia Wei and You-Fa Li. (2017). The Effect of Diaphragmatic Breathing on Attention, Negative Affect and Stress in Healthy Adults. *Frontiers in Psychology*, 8, 874. Published online June 6. DOI:10.3389/fpsyg.2017.00874.

Zaccaro, A., Piarulli, A., Laurino, M., et al. (2018). How Breath-Control Can Change Your Life: A Systematic Review on Psycho-Physiological Correlates of Slow Breathing. *Frontiers in Human Neuroscience* 12, 353. Published online September 7. DOI:10.3389/fnhum.2018.00353.

Zhang Z and Chen W (2018). A Systematic Review of the Relationship between Physical Activity and Happiness. *Journal of Happiness Studies*. DOI:10.1007/s10902-018-9976-0.

5 Where to from here? Making wellbeing comebacks, not wellbeing 'go backs'

While self-compassion, self-care and self-awareness undeniably expand your physical, psychological and emotional wellbeing, they are not the sole determinants of healthy wellbeing. Ages, stages, triumphs, defeats, health, ill health, relationship quality, memories, worries about loved ones and so much more means your wellbeing can fluctuate.

Impeccable, unshakeable and completely consistent wellbeing is a myth, just as impeccable, unshakeable and consistent resilience is.

Respond to wellbeing fluctuations with acceptance and understanding. You know what works for you. You know you're doing your best. Maintaining wellbeing is like growing a muscle. Just because you *want* to grow it doesn't make it *easy* to grow. It's reasonable to not respond to a wellbeing plummet with a wellbeing solution every time. Sometimes you need to stop and do nothing. Take it in. Give it time. What worked one day might not work the next. You might be feeling at the peak of progress and then experience a setback. Don't take these stumbling blocks and your progress personally. Every step towards resetting, recharging and recovering your wellbeing matters. Honour your efforts and intentions. Take your time. Wellbeing will return.

All these unexpected twists and turns are also opportunities for growth and evolution. After experiencing them, your mind and body will not simply bounce back to the way things were. You will have stretched yourself psychologically and changed in some unique way. After any setback, minor or major, your comeback will be with new information and skills you didn't have previously. People are always changing. You're not the same person you were when you were a child, a teenager or at an earlier stage of adulthood. You have adapted and adjusted to everything that's happened around you. Like fine wine, you improve with age.

If the deep insights that emerged during the challenges of the Global Pandemic aren't used for growth in the Education sector, then the period afterwards isn't a comeback, it's a 'go back.' We must collectively do everything we can to not waste this golden opportunity for collaborating around new knowledge. We must look to *you*, the Educators, and be guided on what came to light during the pandemic.

> What worked? What didn't? What should be a priority? What shouldn't be a priority? What are we glad to see the back of? What mattered most?

What didn't matter? What did you learn? What were the grey areas? What were the silver linings within the thick grey clouds?

Educators are qualified, skilled and compassionate professionals who know on the deepest level what it means to teach a young person academically, socially and emotionally. There is a collective global knowledge that wasn't available before 2020 that can benefit the future of Education. Educators are the custodians of this crucial insight.

The following pages offer Educators an opportunity to reflect on what they learned not only about Educator Wellbeing during the pandemic but also about Education. Mostly, this chapter offers a healthy suite of wellbeing strategies to complement previous chapters. It will offer personal growth and self-awareness tools that contribute to a strong foundation, to remain buoyant with any new setbacks that will inevitably come your way.

Final thoughts on the impact of a crisis/the Global Pandemic on Education and Educator wellbeing

Change, obstacles and the element of surprise are not unique to a crisis or pandemic. They are inevitable in school communities and Educators are used to facing and handling them. What a shared crisis does that's different to every day changes, obstacles and surprises is to point everyone's attention towards the same problem, uniting one and all to navigate the same beast.

Before looking ahead to lay the last, interconnecting parts of your wellbeing foundation, it's time to think about what you learned about your wellbeing, Educator wellbeing and Education during the Global Pandemic. If you are new to Education and did not experience the pandemic, you can either listen to what your peers have to say, express what you observed or hypothetically consider this question.

Take journals and paper out to answer the following questions:

What did you learn about your own wellbeing at the start, middle and end of the Global Pandemic?
What did you notice about Educator wellbeing at the start, middle and end of the Global Pandemic?
What worked when teaching went online?
What didn't work about online teaching?
What did the pandemic highlight as necessary in Education?
What did the pandemic highlight as unnecessary in Education?
What changes would you suggest in Education following the experience of the pandemic?
What would you suggest are the lessons to take from the pandemic?

After answering the questions, meet as a group to discuss and create a space for collective wisdom to be shared. Note the patterns in your knowledge.

What's new to you? What had you already considered? What can you all learn from each other? What can be utilised to benefit your school community? How?

While a diverse range of professionals are necessary to advise on Education, never underestimate the sacred knowledge of a hands-on Educator. Whether you're a leader, school support officer, teacher, wellbeing leader, school counsellor or psychologist, your input in the culture and practices in your school community are crucial.

> How might your school community incorporate more input from Educators and balance it with existing policy and Education norms?
> Where is there flexibility in your culture to talk more openly about what is and isn't working in the day-to-day, hands-on work of Educators?
> How can this deep and rich knowledge be listened to and valued?
> How can this information be translated into the academic, social, emotional and wellbeing curriculum?

While there are no easy answers to any of these questions, opening up a dialogue and remembering where significant knowledge lies is a valuable start.

Come back to your purpose in Education

The working life of an Educator is uniquely busy and diverse. Many of you may feel like you're running on autopilot. It's easy to start drawing a blank on why you're in the profession you've chosen. A sense of purpose can help get you through those tough, thankless days. Remembering that you didn't choose Education for recognition and appreciation. You chose it for something way bigger and much deeper than that.

Take a moment to answer the following questions:

> What led you to a career in Education?
> What strengths do you bring to Education?
> What do you want to be known and valued for in Education?
> Why do you work so hard for your students?

Revisit your purpose often. On the days you're overwhelmed and exhausted, you can draw strength from your purpose. Educators impact on students in ways that have a ripple effect long after an Educator has finished teaching or supporting them. Educators pass on kindness, wisdom, confidence and trust to their students, who in turn will pass this on to others. This ripple effect might not be visible right at that moment, or even in the year you teach them – maybe not even for several years because young brains take time to consolidate what you lead them towards. But one day your impact will be clear and it will continue making an impact for generations to come.

See challenges as coaching and make the comeback of your life

Challenges can contribute to long-term growth, when you learn to see them as a unique form of 'coaching.' In the heat of a challenge, the last thing anyone wants to do is think about 'what the lesson is.' Difficulties will consume your energy and continue to exist either way. If you can make their presence somehow useful to you, the new knowledge you obtain through a growth mindset like this can extend you far beyond what might have been possible when everything was running smoothly. Viewing challenges as learning or coaching opportunities frees you from a state of resistance, where you're using all your energy to wish the challenge away or reflect back on when things were 'better.'

Think of the last time you struggled with a student or class dynamic. It was excruciatingly hard wasn't it? Yet, you probably came out of it with far more knowledge than you went in.

You will naturally try and make sense of any challenge you experience. Why not make sense of it by seeing what unexpected gifts it may have brought you?

Here's how

Once you've had your moment, felt the feeling and accepted the arrival of your latest Educator challenge, see if there is something you can learn (or maybe, there is an unexpected gift). Could the challenge prepare you for your next unexpected turn? Could it bring you knowledge or skills you could use to benefit yourself and others? Is it a step closer to your long-term goals as an Educator?

A *functional* relationship with challenge means you seek a purpose for your obstacles and look for ways it might help you. While hard to notice at the time, when you look back on most hardship, you gained something you may not have had without that bump in the road. If everything went consistently smooth, you might not reach far enough out of your comfort zone to experience the necessary growth to progress on your path.

Think back to the three biggest challenges of your life.

> What were they?
> What did you learn about yourself and your life during this time?

Answers can be done privately or in peer mentoring pairs during a staff meeting. Consider creating time during every staff meeting for sharing challenges from the last seven days and what the unexpected gift or new knowledge was. If there isn't much time, suggest everyone write them down as they occur and post them in a box or jar. Pull out one a week to discuss and help keep everyone in tune with this style of thinking.

Next time you're in the sting of a setback, remember it may carry a lesson, tuition and coaching that can help you make a strong comeback and come out better than you went in.

- Can you begin a habit of seeing challenges as a step closer to where you want to be, rather than a step further away?
- Can you start seeing something good in the hardships you face as an Educator?
- Is there good that comes out of having to think on your toes?
- Where might you be as an Educator if everything went smoothly every day and you didn't have to think on your toes?

Don't wait unnecessarily to have 'everything just right' before you take action; you can make progress even in the midst of chaos without having everything in place as planned

When you're a busy Educator, you're used to being organised, prepared for anything and confident in what you're doing. When it comes to trying new things – getting out of your comfort zone, setting goals and doing something for your wellbeing – you might find it harder to get started, wanting the timing to be just right and have 'all your ducks in a row.' While sometimes you absolutely need to wait, have more insight, gain more systems and be more prepared, waiting too long to take your first steps can make it harder for you to progress over time. There is rarely a 'perfect' moment to start something new or work on something that matters to you. There are always obstacles to overcome and work through and, often, they come when you least expect it. Part of wellbeing (and making a comeback) is taking healthy and calculated risks so you can see yourself come out the other end stronger and closer to what you want and need.

Think of something you want to achieve in Education

Do you want to write a blog or a book? Increase awareness about something that matters to you? Engage in further study? Learn more about a particular topic? Find a mentor?

- What is one small step you can take to move closer towards it **today**?
- What are five small steps, one a day that will take you closer to your goal over the next **week**?

Every step, no matter how small, is important. Breaking plans down into manageable chunks will make starting and staying on track infinitely easier.

Avoid making big decisions under pressure

Hardships like the Global Pandemic pushed many Educators so far over the edge they thought about quitting. They wouldn't normally think so reactively, but these weren't normal circumstances.

The immediate, overwhelming and unexpected pressure that came with the pandemic threw everyone into a spin. No matter how calm and together you may have gone into it, everyone felt unravelled by the end of it. Even if you weren't directly affected, seeing the world face such uncertainty placed pressure on everyone. Educators bore a big brunt of pressure as did many others. When something this unexpected and life altering happens, it's difficult to think straight and remain calm. We saw many private practice Educators who had lost business during the social distancing measures rush to invest in developing online programmes only to see the market saturated quickly by others who were one step ahead or had much larger budgets to play with.

When you're under pressure and feeling overwhelmed sometimes the best thing you can do for your wellbeing is pause. Don't take action; sit for a bit. When life feels like an emergency, it's important to step out of the emergency lane for a moment, gather some perspective and slow down. When you avoid jumping on every fear-based impulse and reaction, your heart rate and breathing calms down, switching the clear-thinking part of your brain back on. Making big decisions *only* after you've had time to think, discuss and sit with it supports your psychological wellbeing.

As an Educator, you might need to regulate this not only for yourself but also for your students. If a young person is really struggling and you're feeling overwhelmed, give yourself and the situation some space and time. You might feel pressured to, but you don't have to solve it immediately. If you receive an upsetting email, try not to respond straight away when your feelings are rumbling. Give time for the dust to settle. Think carefully about how you might respond in a neutral way.

Someone dear taught me years ago, when I struggled to say 'no' to helping anyone and everyone who needed me (at the sacrifice of my own time and wellbeing), to confidently say 'I'll think about that and get back to you really soon.' Learning to use 'I'll think about that' provides you with some thinking time (which you're entitled to) so you can ascertain clearly whether or not the request is within your capacity. You can care deeply about someone and a situation and still hold your personal boundaries close and say 'no.'

Adapt to change

Responding to change with flexibility and adaptability improves your coping ability. Change is hard on everyone, especially when you've settled into comfortable routine. Few people embrace change and most, at least initially, resist it. Educators are used to it – their environments are often changing. Developing tools to not only accept it but to adapt with it is that part that's often left out.

Learning how to think outside your comfort zone and flexibly adapt to change takes some time. Adapting to change is a healthy and functional way of regaining some control where it was lost.

As a group, answer the following questions in relation to your school community. Alternatively, answer them privately or in peer mentoring groups/pairs.

In what ways have you been adaptable in the past?
What strengths do you have that help you adapt to difficulties?
What is the most uncomfortable part of adapting?
What are some of the positive emotions that come out of adapting to change?
Change will come whether you like it or not. Will you resist or adapt?

Step in and out of your comfort zone

While plenty of growth can happen while you're safe and snug inside your comfort zone, being pushed out of your comfort zones calls on skills like courage, confidence, resilience, creativity, flexibility and adaptability, all of which contribute to psychological wellbeing and flourishing. Stepping *out* of your comfort zone is only part of the solution. Make sure you step back *in* too, to rest, recover and reflect. Often, I see well intended affirmations telling people to step *out* of the comfort zone, failing to recognise this is not only hard, but impossible to sustain consistently, every day of your life. Our personalities and abilities are all on a spectrum and there are many different comfort zones we may hold on to. A person who happily gets strapped to a rock-climbing harness and takes off on a cliffside adventure one day might find a party with a group of unknown people thoroughly agonising the next day. We all have different strengths, abilities and comfort zones. Try not to measure how often you step out against how often others step out, and always remember you're allowed to step back in.

Look back often at how far you've come

When you find yourself looking at the long road ahead, remember to look back on how far you've already come. Throughout your career, you've overcome so much. As an Educator, your job can be stressful, unpredictable and overwhelming. Acknowledge how well you've navigated your work. Appreciate and value where you have already grown instead of solely focusing on where you need to grow. Honour your progress.

Think of three times in your career as an Educator where there was a closed door or unexpected turn in the road and things did not go according to plan. For each situation, try and answer the following questions in your journal or through a peer mentoring conversation.

How did you evolve and grow?
What skills did you develop because of the need to adapt and respond?
What growth did you experience that you might not have experienced if you hadn't gone through this?

Consciously congratulate yourself and your resilience. Along the winding path, you have grown and evolved and, mostly likely, made something good come from it.

Avoid falling into the cultural trap of looking after your students 'no matter what'

When you're an Educator, you're most likely dedicated, kind and compassionate, choosing your profession because young people's education, mental health and wellbeing matter to you. A question I've always asked in my work with Educators was magnified with the global impact of the pandemic and here it is:

> At what cost are Educators caring for others?

Education is deeply valued and necessary across the globe. Yet Educators, who provide the education, report that despite the satisfaction they gain from the positive impact they're making, they are concurrently exhausted, overwhelmed, feel under supported and even burnt out. Many are reluctantly leaving a profession they studied and worked hard for as a last resort to manage excessive stress.

Educators carry out a complex juggling act of teaching, nurturing, leading, adapting the curriculum, communicating with colleagues, leadership and parents, responding to unexpected challenges and much more – often all in one day. No one is doing this *to you* on purpose. It's that your work, while satisfying and interesting, is also emotionally taxing, demanding and well and truly matters. Educators tend to have the kind of personality that will do anything for their students even if it costs them their own wellbeing.

It's time to end putting yourself last. You can be a brilliant Educator even if your boundaries shift to allow for self-care. You can be a kind person and say 'no.' You can be resilient and need help. You can be a sensational leader and not know all the answers. You can care about your work and desperately want a rest.

Approach the norms of 'do whatever it takes for your student's learning and wellbeing' with caution. You matter, too. You deserve a joyful and balanced life that leaves your heart and mind full in ways that are beyond your role as an Educator.

Take a moment to journal what aspects of your work as an Educator is pushing you to your limits. Next to each challenge, answer the following questions:

> At what cost you are rising to this challenge?
> What are your top three challenges right now?
> Can these be outsourced, supported or removed from your priorities?

This isn't an easy task and I strongly advise you to do it with a friend, colleague or support person.

Work out what matters to you, then do what you can to make it happen

When you work in Education, it can become a strong part of your personal identity. What you do is not 'just a job.' It's so much more. A little like you might hear parents say they don't remember who they were and what they did before they became parents, I hear a similar conversation from many Educators.

It's important you don't let your work be the only place you hold your value.

By focusing your free time on other pursuits that have nothing to do with Education, you're strengthening your foundation so you're more able to appreciate and enjoy the work you do so well.

> Take your journal out and 'flood' it with every little (and big) value, pastime and pursuit that matters to you.
> What makes your heart sing? What makes your mind dance? What brings your soul to life?

Now share this with a friend, confidant or colleague. Express this part of you that goes beyond your unconditional willingness to serve your students. I have worked in schools where Educators have had discussions about their wellbeing needs and personal interests, written them on a card and displayed them in the staff room. This made checking in on each other's interests and plans for better wellbeing more naturally part of the conversation.

And here's the trickiest but doable part:

> What's your plan to make what matters to you count and bring it into your life again?

Always have something to look forward to, no matter how small

Having hope and joy in what's ahead can bring hope and joy in the moment now. While it's exciting to have a big overseas or interstate holiday to look forward to, not all of us are afforded this kind of luxury. As we learned all too recently through the pandemic, even with a plan to travel ahead of you, sometimes borders close and plane travel comes to a halt. We can't rely solely on our 'escapes' for our wellbeing.

Looking forward to and savouring small events as well big ones brings on feelings of anticipation that strengthen your wellbeing. Write a list of all the small pleasures in your life – from your favourite cup of coffee to the feeling you get after exercise, to the laughter a conversation with a treasured friend brings. Make a list so long that you will find at least one (and hopefully many more) things to look forward to every day. When you walk into your staff room or classroom each morning bring at least a couple of these to mind and remind yourself about what you're looking forward to. Imagine yourself enjoying it. Know the moment is not far away.

Have goals and write them down

Psychologist Gail Matthews's (2015) research demonstrated that when people wrote down their goals they were 33 percent more successful in achieving them than those who formulated outcomes in their heads.

Before looking ahead and planning, begin by looking back and celebrating how far you've come as an Educator. Reflecting back on your efforts is like experiencing them all over again and an important reminder of your capability and confidence to achieve what you set out to.

> Summarise the goals you have previously set and reached so far.
> Acknowledge the small steps you achieved along the way.

Notice how many short-term goals led you towards your bigger, long-term ones.

> Are your goals reflecting what matters to you?

You're more likely to achieve goals when they are meaningful to you and set by your genuine desire to reach them. Many adults find themselves in careers, hobbies and lifestyles that have nothing to do with their own interests. They have been living someone else's dream. They followed what they were encouraged to as children and what they felt would please others.

Your wellbeing is more likely to thrive when your goals align with your purpose and what's personally meaningful and joyful to you. It might take some time to redefine these and some of them need to stay, in order to sustain your livelihood and connections with others.

Take some time to answer the following questions:

> What goals were you encouraged to reach as a child, teenager and young adult?
> Which of these goals are most meaningful to you now?
> Which ones did you reach?
> What personal and professional goals do you genuinely want to reach in the next month?
> What personal and professional goals do you genuinely want to reach in the next 12 months?

Goal scan and audit: are your goals the right goals for where you're at right now?

For goals to be achievable, they need to be right for your mindset, skills and role in Education at the time. It's great to have bigger, long-term goals of course, but it's important to be realistic. It's also necessary to make sure your goals are broken up into smaller, manageable goals within a short time frame while you build confidence. Rushing too quickly can lead to early burnout and a loss of interest. This does not mean you don't dream big; you must imagine the best for yourself. When it comes to getting there, you need to allow for the small steps along the way as well as the setbacks.

Review your goals from the previous activity. Rank them in order of which are presently closest to your interests, current mindset and skill level. Take your time to choose one at a time, break it down into smaller, achievable steps, make a plan to work towards it a little each day. Be patient with yourself. Your wellbeing will suffer if this exercise turns into frustration and disappointment with yourself for not reaching your goals. If it's not the right time, do something else and come back to it later.

Know yourself as a person – not only as an Educator

Many people skip this step when working on their wellbeing and making a comeback from a setback. Know myself? What does that even mean? We all have a unique personality and sense of what feels right and wrong. Sometimes in Education, a career that can err on the side of all consuming, you might forget who that is. You might become lost in seeing your role as an Educator as who you are. Sometimes, because you had to fit in with someone else's expectations, you lost sight of who that was in the first place.

To know yourself, you need to have the courage to face yourself for exactly who you are.

Here are some questions you can ask yourself to get started:

1 If you had to tell someone about yourself in 10 words or less, which words would you use to describe yourself?
2 What are five things that matter most to you?
3 What lesson is hardest for you to learn – even though you know it's good for you?
4 What do you add to the room when you enter?
5 How do you want to be remembered?

Find your strengths and use them

Educators have unique strengths. All too often, I see them focus more on where they struggle and what their imperfections are than where they are progressing. Engaging in your strengths and talents is an essential part of nurturing your self-esteem and wellbeing (Du, King and Chi 2017).

Using your strengths and talents promotes physiological changes in your brain associated with happiness. It also enhances your connection to others, bringing meaning and purpose while strengthening your sense of self (Mental Health Foundation 2012).

Take a moment to write down your main strengths

Try not to focus on achievement-oriented strengths and, instead, focus on your character. You might prefer to work this out through an evidence-based survey like www.viacharacter.org, which will assess your character strengths and place them in order from strongest to weakest. This can be a helpful self-awareness tool to remind you of all the things you can be proud of.

People who are aware of and use their strengths are likely to feel more energised and well than people who focus on their challenges and weaknesses.

Share vulnerability

Most Educators see their role as a kind of sacred duty towards the future wellbeing and success of their students. Being in a position which matters so much and carries the potential for influencing others and the world also comes with an unwritten pressure to be 'perfect.' You might feel like you can't make mistakes or *not* know what to do. The good news for you cutting yourself some slack is that, when people seem super human without any flaws, this lack of vulnerability and imperfection can make it difficult for others to relate to you. Having some flaws and vulnerabilities not only make you human, they make you relatable. When you know you don't have to hide these, it's much easier to be authentic and relax.

1 What are three of your most loveable vulnerabilities or imperfections as an Educator?
2 What are three of your less loveable vulnerabilities or imperfections as an Educator?

After you have recognised these, acknowledge and accept them. Allow their presence. Let a glimpse of them be seen every now and again. You're human. This is an excellent activity to do in peer mentoring pairs and groups, or as a whole staff, to strengthen the social thread in the school community.

Ask for advice, a favour or some kind of help every now and again

Most Educators I've worked with are willing and happy to help others. Whether it's an opportunity to give advice, do a favour or assist in some way, they enjoy feeling valuable and useful. Every time you help or receive help, you're bonding and connecting with another person. When you ask a friend for advice, a favour or help, you're not only showing you're human and can't do it all alone but you're showing that you appreciate them and their skills and knowledge.

What are some areas you could enlist your friends' advice, favours or help?

Asking for help is not a weakness; it's a sign of courage and is a wellbeing necessity.

Understand the social media comparison trap and limit your involvement

Social media can be a great place to connect, follow what you're interested in and share what you care about. It's important to keep in perspective, however, that social media is only a snapshot of other people's experiences. When you're on social media for longer than necessary, it can feel like other Educators are more competent than you. It can also look like they are having an endlessly good time and aren't being met with the same challenges as you are. When you look inside their classrooms or eyeball their strategies, you can feel like you're falling behind. Your work doesn't have to be 'Instagram-worthy' to be worthy.

What works for them might not work for you. Their students have different needs than yours. Their school is different from yours. The supports they have in place are different. The list is endless.

Try following social media accounts that are neutral or positive, instead of just colleagues, friends, other Educators or Education experts. Art, animals, nature and travel destinations are all examples of neutral interests you can follow to balance what you're looking at.

> Take a moment to look at your social media accounts. Pay conscious attention to how you feel and what you think as you scroll. Is there anything you're following that is unravelling you emotionally? Can you unfollow it for a while? What uplifts you? Can you add that as a 'favourite' so it's always the first thing you see?

Only reply to a message when you're in a good or neutral mood

Why is this a wellbeing tool? I sometimes see Educators get overwhelmed and defensively react to an email or text message that has upset them. They reply too quickly, before their emotions have had time to settle. This can leads to regret and sleepless nights, which in turn affects wellbeing.

When you receive an upsetting message, learn to walk away from your device and do something calming with those difficult feelings. Come back to the message when you're feeling better – or even better, come back the next day. Working in a field that involves the wellbeing and growth of young people can mean you find yourself unfairly judged or even criticised sometimes. When a child is struggling, people have a tendency to put pressure on Educators to 'fix it' or be accountable for something that is out of their hands. This means they might say things that are unintentionally hurtful. How you respond is important and your best chance of responding in a balanced way you won't regret is with time.

Kindness as a core value

A single daily random act of kindness can improve your sense of happiness and wellbeing (Cutler 2018). Being kind and generous has also been shown to activate a part of the brain called the *striatum*, which responds to pleasure from rewarding experiences (Jorge et al. 2006).

Kindness comes more naturally when you're feeling balanced and on top of everything. People have infinitely more emotional resources to extend to others when not consumed with mental clutter, personal challenges and an extensive to-do list. No one can be consistently kind without exception either. Start with the intention to be kind, then allow yourself room for error on days when you only have the energy to be kind to yourself.

Kindness can be as simple as not joining in gossip, complimenting someone others have rejected, wishing someone luck for something that's important to them, picking some fruit or flowers from your home to share with colleagues, baking a cake for staff meeting, complimenting a colleague on their teaching style, making a newcomer feel welcome or smiling and listening intently.

Doing a kind thing for another person every day is a simple and effective way to improve your wellbeing. When you're going through a challenge, you might not feel like it and it's okay to take a break. Funnily enough, when you're down it is an ideal time to step out of your personal difficulty and reach out to another person in kindness. A grateful and empathic exchange often follows an act of kindness that might just be what you need to feel uplifted.

Find your legacy

Leaving a legacy is one way to mark the world with your contribution. When you start to think about how you want to be remembered, you will want people to see your life as instrumental in some way. As Educators, you leave your legacy in every student you teach, imparting values of learning, compassion, connection, effort, persistence and so forth.

An Educator's legacy continues on in their students much longer than you might realise. Educator contribution can have an ongoing, positive impact on a young person's wellbeing. The mark you leave on a student gets passed on to others in the young person's life. It really is one of the most profound legacies you can have.

Being an Educator however, should not be your only legacy. Your role is meaningful, fulfilling and inspiring to others, but there is still more to you.

Take a moment to answer the following questions to try and identify another legacy you wish to leave as a footprint on other people's lives long after you're gone.

- What do you care most about that has nothing to do with your job?
- Where do your personal strengths, character and values already have an impact and influence?
- How do you want to be remembered?
- What steps (no matter how small) can you take to find and build your legacy?

Not everyone will know what their legacy is yet. Good things take time and it might not be your time yet to know. It will come to you and when it does, hear the call and soar.

Plan to be responsible for your health

When you're a child, your parents and carers contribute significantly to your health by leading you towards healthy eating, moving and wellbeing habits. Once you reach teenage years and adulthood, your health becomes your responsibility even when no one is watching.

When you work in Education, time is often at a premium. You need to be prepared for each day outside of the hours that you're teaching and supporting. You can't afford to arrive unprepared, as your students need your leadership and are almost always with you. Even when they are not directly with you, an Educator is always supervising and monitoring engagement and connection. Making time to prepare a nutritious breakfast and lunch when you leave home early and often finish late can make nutrition challenging. By the time you get home, it might be tempting to eat whatever you can get your hands on or order take away.

Carefully choosing how you treat your health and valuing yourself enough to beneficially nourish your body is a learned skill. Be patient with yourself as you learn to navigate this. Be conscious about how you treat your body, seeing it as a valuable instrument that needs dedicated care to survive and thrive. Appreciate your body for its heartbeat, breath and ability to move you around to where you want to be. Without being unnecessarily vigilant, think carefully about what you put into it. Try and move it enough, rest it enough and nourish it enough.

While there are often complex reasons why caring for health is challenging for some, nurturing your health will help uphold and strengthen your wellbeing. Seek help to get it on track if you're struggling. Teaming up with a friend, partner or colleague is another way to set some goals and have a sense of accountability around them.

Forgive yourself on those days you are too indulgent – it's okay to have those, too.

- What are some healthy rituals you would like to do more of to take care of your health?
- Is there a way to incorporate it into your class's health and wellbeing curriculum?

Engaging in lifelong learning

During the Global Pandemic, many people found themselves attending online classes they never had time to attend previously, discovering a long-lost love of learning. Learning new skills is energising and exciting. Now that the pandemic is over doesn't mean you have to stop the fun you were having online. Consider investing in your wellbeing by attending a class on a topic you've always wanted to learn but have struggled to find time for.

Organise your space and declutter every few months

This isn't about being excessively or unreasonably neat or keeping a home that's picture perfect. It's about maintaining the space around you well enough so that looking for your belongings isn't a constant difficulty and you're not holding on to more than is necessary.

Some suggest spending five minutes on each room of your home every day to give it a quick tidy up before you sit down for your evening rest. This is often the last thing hard working Educators feel they have the energy for, yet those who have made the commitment to doing it experience a sense of wellbeing when they wake up in the morning without an immediate assault of 'things to do' in front of them.

A tidy, decluttered and organised environment can lead to rest and wellbeing in your mind.

Understanding alienation to enhance belonging and wellbeing

Your connection to yourself, your work, others and nature provides you with a foundation that supports your healthy wellbeing. Karl Marx's theory of alienation continues to have validity in current day society, where the pace and increased connection through devices rather than face-to-face contact can sometimes get in the way of meaningful connections. Alienation simply means being a stranger to something (Istvan Meszaros 1970). The four areas Marx referred to are stated below.

1. *Alienation from nature.*
   Disconnecting from nature and spending too much time indoors can be stifling. Time spent in the natural world has the potential to significantly reduce stress and improve wellbeing. Time in nature costs nothing and is easily accessible. Even when the weather is less favourable, you can access nature through the view from a window.

2. *Alienation from others.*
   Spending too much time alone and away from other people leaves you with little more than your own company, your own thoughts and your own perspective. Spending time face to face with other people helps balance the way you see yourself, others and the world.

3. *Alienation from work.*
   Work has many purposes. The obvious one is it provides income. Work that is meaningful to you and has a purpose contributes to healthy wellbeing. If you're only working in a job because it's something you're good at or because you know it is a necessary field but your heart isn't in it, you're likely to become alienated from it. This contributes to lower satisfaction with your life. It might help to think back to why you chose Education in the first place.

4   *Alienation from ourselves.*
    Feelings, intuition and thoughts are there for a reason. They are part of being human. We are wired to connect to ourselves and others. Ignoring our feelings and not investing in yourself and your personal growth makes you a stranger to yourself. Reconnecting to your intuition, your values, your feelings and your perspective is crucial for your wellbeing.

Take a moment to think of how you can meet these four needs in your life more often. How can you prioritise them as much as you prioritise your students' wellbeing and learning outcomes?

Create a space between what happens around you and your reactions

Quick, impulsive reactions are only natural when someone says or does something out of the blue that makes you feel uncomfortable.

Creating a space between yourself, your reactions and what happens around you is an important life skill that will help you avoid saying something you regret in the heat of the moment. One way you can do this is by imagining you're physically surrounded by something you find peaceful and beautiful; perhaps a rainbow, a field of flowers or fluffy white clouds. Imagine that no matter what someone says or does, their words and actions can't enter beyond that space of peace around you. Within your peaceful space, you pause, breathe and centre yourself before responding. Counting to ten in your mind while in this space can help you slow down, too. Making a conscious decision to be calm in chaos also helps. Like with anything, don't be hard on yourself if you don't achieve what you set out to every time. Humans naturally struggle with maintaining equanimity when they feel confronted.

Staying peaceful and composed during problems and decision making

Poise (your ability to remain peaceful, composed and neutral) is vital for healthy wellbeing. Poise supports productive problem solving and decision making by helping you sustain a sense of peace during emotional storms. It's about being the point of clarity and calm despite how others behave around you.

Educators are frequently confronted by young people's high needs and emotions. It is especially important Educators have the tools to not react or absorb their student's emotions. Adding one emotional storm to another will always make things worse. By learning to regulate your feelings and not react to provocation, you are contributing to a crucial part of your emotional intelligence and wellbeing, while supporting your students' growth, too.

Maintaining poise is initially a conscious decision. After that, it's about looking after yourself, managing your stress and maintaining your wellbeing enough that you can be calmer and maintain poise easier. You're infinitely more likely to manage your feelings with poise if you're taking care of yourself.

Movement

Movement is an essential part of wellbeing and one that can be hard to start and make time for. Not everyone feels motivated to move even though we all know it's important for health and wellbeing. Try answering the following questions:

- What gets in the way of being active?
- What might help you be more active?
- How do you feel after you have been active?
- How do you feel when you haven't been active?
- If you were to add some time for movement in your day, what might be the best time?
- If you were to add some movement to your day, what are the most enjoyable ways you like to move?
- Could you get started by setting the goal to get up on the hour, every hour you're awake and take a moment to walk around your house, classroom or garden?

Educators tend to be quite active in their work, but it's still important to find movement that is just for you, is structured and gets your heart rate up. Difficult thoughts and emotions can build up quickly, generating excessive energy and feelings of unrest. Around 30 minutes of exercise a day can have a similar outcome to taking antidepressants for a person with mild to moderate depression. Other benefits in the same study showed increased protection against heart disease and diabetes as well as improved sleep and lower blood pressure. A meta-analysis of 455 patients by the University of Thessaly in Greece found exercising for 20–30 minutes each day reduces anxiety and depression (Morres et al. 2018).

Empathy: putting yourself in someone else's shoes

One of the most valuable skills in emotional intelligence is being able to put yourself in another person's shoes. Staying caught in your own mind and experiences can mean you'll go over and over thoughts that are not necessarily helpful.

Empathy increases social harmony, improves mental health and contributes to stronger relationships. Studies have shown people with empathy have greater personal and professional success, higher levels of happiness, better relationships and lower stress (Post and Neimark 2008).

As an Educator you're often confronted with a young person's unbridled emotions and perspectives. Seeing things from their perspective can make it easier not to react as you tune in to their inexperience and vulnerability, reminded that their knowledge and skills are still developing. Research has shown how empathy assists emotional regulation at times of confrontation (Pace et al. 2009). It's much easier to remain calm once you've left your own state of mind and compassionately entered someone else's.

Nurture optimism

Optimistic Educators know school environments are often a handful, and conflict and challenge are inevitable from time to time. They are not blind enthusiasts who think everything works out no matter what. They remain rational and realistic. Optimistic Educators are great observers. Their capacity to stay calm through balanced analysis and maintain a positive outlook is a valuable skill, and one that gives them an advantage over others in times of crisis and conflict. Optimists acknowledge negative events, but are less likely to blame themselves for bad outcomes. They instead tend to view the situation as a temporary one, and expect further positive events to come into their future.

As you practice a new mindset like optimism, be patient and allow yourself to struggle with it. You can choose an hour a day to begin with, perhaps in class with your students, where you make the intention to be optimistic about your ability to teach well and your student's ability to learn well.

Spend time in friendly company

Social connection is a primary contributing factor to happiness and good health. Relationship quality is important. Spending large amounts of time with unhappy or negative people is not without its consequences. While you can't avoid personalities with a negative outlook or disposition, it's important to understand how easily pessimistic attitudes are absorbed, even if you have high levels of optimism yourself. Research has shown that the impact of being around unhappy people negatively effects your cardiovascular and mental health (Friedman and Martin 2012).

Identify Educators in your workplace that are optimistic, kind and uplifting. These are the colleagues whose words and actions you need to absorb and relate yourself with. Spend time with them. Support them. Create a self-protection plan for people who are the opposite. Limit time spent with pessimists or trouble makers, manage stress before and after seeing them and use encouraging and positive self-talk to cope. Seeing the person through the eyes of compassion can also be helpful; however, this can be harder in the short term if the person is being intentionally hurtful or challenging.

Social connection is vital for happiness stability and maintaining a healthy emotional state. Remain in tune with the kind of friendships and connections you foster.

Do the inner work: sanguine

If you're looking for more and have other challenges that are troubling you or inhibiting your wellbeing progress, another of my books, *Sanguine: 21 days to confidence, optimism and self-awareness* (2020) is an accessible and practical self-directed journal designed for adults as well as children and teenagers. You can engage in 'sanguine' on your own, with your family or as a class/whole school approach to building confidence, optimism and self-awareness in staff and students. In just ten minutes a day, answering simple questions, you can delve deeper within to give your wellbeing a final, uplifting boost. It can be found via www.positivemindsaustralia.com.au as a hard copy Australia-wide, or as an ebook site license for whole schools/classes/other groups across Australia and overseas.

Final thoughts

By now you've considered loads of practical wellbeing solutions. You might like all of them, you might like five of them. All that matters now is that you sit for a moment and, without judging yourself, decide what might help give yourself the care you deserve. The right wellbeing tool is the right wellbeing tool for *you*. As you reflect back on what you liked, mark it and adapt it to suit your personality, your role in Education and your life as a whole being.

Use this book as a framework to build a personalised approach to wellbeing that suits your personality and circumstances. Come back here as often as you like, grab a strategy, make it yours and go for it.

Thank you for reading. Thank you for working so hard. Every day your wisdom, persistence, compassion and dedication are impacting the world in ways that can never be measured fully, in ways that matter above and beyond what you may ever realise.

You are the gentle leaders of the next generation.

>   Be you.
>   Be well.
>   Be wonderful.
>
>   It was my absolute privilege to write this for you.
>   With very best wishes to all of you, always,
>   Madhavi Nawana Parker

References

Cutler J and Banerjee R (2018). Five Reasons Why Being Kind Makes You Feel Good - According to Science. *The Conversation*, February 27.

Du, H., King, R. B. and Chi, P. (2017). Self-Esteem and Subjective Well-Being Revisited: The Roles of Personal, Relational, and Collective Self-Esteem. *PLoS One*, 12 (8), e0183958. Published online August 25. DOI:10.1371/journal.pone.0183958.

Friedman, H. S. and Martin, L. R. (2012). *The Longevity Project: Surprising Discoveries for Health and Long Life from the Landmark Eight-Decade Study*. New York Penguin Random House.

Iyer, A. (2017). *Become a More Optimistic Version of Yourself*. Dallas: University of Texas, Southwestern Medical Centre.

Meszaros, I (1970). *Marx's Theory of Alienation*. London: The Merlin Press.
Mental Health Foundation. (2012). *Doing Good Does You Good*, written by Dr Dan Robotham, Isabella Goldie, Lauren Chakkalackal, Chris White, Kirsten Morgan and Dr Eva Cyhlarova.
Moll J et al (2006). Human Fronto-Mesolimbic Networks Guide Decisions about Charitable Donation, *Proceedings of the National Academy of Sciences of the United States of America (PNAS)* 103, no. 42 15623–15628.
Morres ID, Hatzigeorgiadis, A, Stathi, A, Comoutos, N, Arpin-Cribbie C, Krommidas, C and Theodorakis, Y (2018). Aerobic Exercise for Adult Patients with Major Depressive Disorder in Mental Health Services: A Systematic Review and Meta-analysis. *Depression and Anxiety Journal* 36 no. 1.
Pace, T. W. W., Negi, L. T., Adame, D. D., Cole, S. P., Sivilli, T. I., Brown, T. D., Issa, M. J. and Raison, C. L. (2009). Effect of Compassion Meditation on Neuroendocrine, Innate Immune and Behavioural Responses to Psychosocial Stress. *Psychoneuroendocrinolgy*, 34, 87–98.
Post, S. G. and Neimark, J. (2008). *Why Good things Happen to Good People: The Exciting New Research That Proves the Link between Doing Good and Living a Long, Healthier, Happier Life*. New York: Broadway Books.

6 Stories of courage, hope and endurance

Wellbeing during crisis and challenge

This chapter is based on the life changing moments of every day folks who have experienced an unexpected crisis or tragedy and somehow found ways to reset, recover and recharge to support their wellbeing. It was my privilege to interview them. May their stories inspire and remind you that recovery and wellbeing take time; efforts are not completely straightforward.

Sometimes, to make sense of the ups and downs of life and find morsels of hope amongst the tragedy and unfairness, you must look in the simplest of places.

Perhaps these are just the stories to bring comfort and reassurance that in time, when you're ready, there is *always* something you *can* do, even when there's so much you *can't*.

Maybe you will see some part of yourself in a story that, while different to yours, may resonate and uplift you.

Or if nothing more, you will be reminded of the beauty and fragility of life and how every day on this earth with our loved ones is indeed a precious gift without any promise of another day.

Warning: The following stories contain detailed accounts of extreme personal difficulties as well as tragedies. Please read at your own discretion.

Dr Gill Hicks, AM MBE, founding director M.A.D for Peace, counter-terrorism expert, keynote speaker, author, artist and curator (www.musicartdiscussion.com)

Gill Hicks, peace advocate, motivational speaker, author, artist and curator, is also the founder of the London-based not-for-profit organisation MAD [Music, Art, Discussion] for Peace. Early on the morning of 7 July 2005, Gill boarded a London train carriage at the same time as a 19-year-old bomber. Moments later, multiple explosions ripped through the London underground train network. Gill lost both legs instantly, sustaining multiple permanent injuries. Plunged into darkness, her survival hung on by a thread. Resourcefully, Gill removed her scarves, creating a tourniquet for her legs and consciously slowing her breathing down. Slipping in and out of consciousness, Gill fought the urge to close her eyes. With a courage and determination Gill is famous for, she repeated the mantra 'This is not the place I will die.'

Gill arrived in hospital with most of her blood lost. She had been clinically dead for 28 minutes. Her hospital band stated 'one unknown, estimated female.' This tiny band was instrumental in her response and recovery from that moment. Who Gill was, her gender, ethnicity, faith or social status didn't matter to her first responders. They unquestioningly put their lives at risk in that dreadful underground horror scene to save hers. Holding her hand, not letting go once, stroking her face gently and surrounding her with love and compassion, Gill experienced firsthand the transformative effect of unconditional love, compassion, connection and respect. Gill has honoured and translated this experience and knowledge across the globe ever since.

A gruelling path of recovery began by drawing a line between her 'first life' and 'second life.' The first was before the bombings. Gill was thriving in a career she loved as head of a department at The Design Council, and Fellow of The Royal Society for the Arts with an already prolific writing portfolio; a young, successful and independent 37-year-old Australian living the dream in London. The second life, as Gill reflects, 'came with a new contract.' A double amputee and survivor, Gill began relentless cycles of rehabilitation, enduring indescribable pain and post-traumatic stress. Determined to bring others together after an attack that divided people, Gill led a walk on prosthetic legs of almost 200 miles from Yorkshire (where three out of the four bombers came from) to London. She invited anyone and everyone from all walks of life to join her and they did. Gill left a high-ranking career and dedicated her 'second life' to advocate for peace, love, compassion and counter-terrorism.

Gill found a way to take what she had learned from that tragic day to find a purpose for herself and others, changing peoples' perspectives around the world about counter-terrorism, life, art and beyond.

There are ample days that are gruelling and painful. Gill recalls times like the day on a tiny rural plane to Karratha, Western Australia, early in her 'second life,' where she was feeling especially overwhelmed with exhaustion and doubt. Unable to rest comfortably, her legs were hurting terribly. Gill wondered how this new life that she had grown fond of, but came with little predictability, support and validation, was sustainable. She had a great career back in London. She had plans in London. All was well in London. A stranger sitting beside Gill passed her a note at that moment. It read, 'Thank you for advocating for peace and love and asking for more than just tolerance.' Gill tells me that moment is a reminder that even if you don't receive thanks, gratitude exists. She knows her work is changing lives and matters. Gill urges others to stay focused on their success stories, repeating them over in your mind . . . to not get caught in what still needs doing . . . to take time to celebrate the wins and to keep your sources of validation close.

Gill is a beacon for courage, determination, compassion, hope and widespread positive change. Her impact and achievements in both her 'first' and 'second' life seem never-ending. Gill doesn't do things in halves. Her ability to accept the unimaginable, without hatred or a wish for retribution, can't be easy, yet she makes it look effortless.

Gill's six-year-old daughter has strengthened Gill's admiration for the power of Educators, whom she calls 'Futurists,' 'Bastions of Hope' and 'Keepers of Humanity.' Gill encourages Educators to look after their wellbeing by never underestimating their impact as they impart knowledge. To be real, to value themselves, to surround themselves with supportive people and find something that feeds their soul.

Gill is determined to continue her generous, heartfelt and life changing work. She says, 'we're here for a little measure of time – we don't know when we'll go. We have to ask ourselves, "what can I do in that time?"' For Gill, her daughter is her legacy, her work at MAD, her purpose and her art, her soul food – the thread from the first life to the second life, from the moment she met death, until now.

When I asked Gill where her courage, generosity and determination comes from, she told me it was easy . . .

'Because it matters.'

Nicholas Lee, founder and CEO of the Jodi Lee Foundation, accredited mental health first aid instructor, keynote and public speaker (www.jodileefoundation.org.au)

Founder, CEO and chairman of the Jodi Lee Foundation, finalist for Australian of the Year 2015, keynote and public speaker Nick Lee is first and foremost a dedicated father of two. Nick honours his wife, Jodi, who he lost to bowel cancer in 2010, by taking what he learned from his family tragedy into an opportunity for hope for other Australians. By raising their two children with everything he's got and showing them that even in the saddest times there is always something you *can* do, Nick's story is one of resilience, optimism and endurance.

When Jodi was diagnosed with stage 4 bowel cancer, the numbness, disbelief and grief were all consuming. Nick and Jodi had two young children. With little time left together, their joyful, fulfilled and uncomplicated life would never go back to what it was.

Jodi, a doting mother, loving wife and dedicated special needs teacher, accepted her terminal diagnosis long before Nick could bring his heart to it. Nick, an optimist and loyal protector of his family, was still thinking her cancer was a 'decent-sized bump in the road' that she would conquer and he could protect his family from.

Before Jodi's passing, Nick brought her pride and hope for others, with one last act of dedication by raising over $100,000 for the Cancer Council. While caring for Jodi during her gruelling last months, Nick processed his stress by focusing on what he could control.

When Jodi passed away on 16 January 2010 at 41, Nick, now a grieving sole parent of a six- and eight-year-old, felt the world as he knew it fall apart.

With a determined, compassionate and purposeful heart, strong corporate and business background and fundraising success already, Nick left a high-ranking position in the corporate world to dedicate his career and strengths to preventing bowel cancer. Nick wanted nothing more than to prevent others from enduring what Jodi and their family had. Jodi was young, fit and healthy. There was no way to tell she could be facing a terminal diagnosis at 39. Bowel cancer, when detected early, can be cured. The Jodi Lee Foundation was born out of love for Jodi, their two children and for all the other families Nick wanted to protect. The Jodi Lee Foundation fundraises specifically for the prevention of bowel cancer. Nick has done what he set out to; Jodi's tragic loss will never be in vain and her name will never be forgotten.

I asked Nick why, when most people would (understandably) be frozen with grief, he was able to start a foundation, promptly receive a grant over $2.5 million from the federal government, gain support from noteworthy groups like the Australian Football League, and raise hundreds of thousands of dollars through his own efforts, without sacrificing his first priority – his two young children?

Nick, emotionally intelligent and a willing conversationalist, credits much of his ability to reinvent his life in a way that also helped with the grieving process to his family and friends. Nick had support and friendship in abundance. Being a friend and having empathy has always been one of Nick's greatest strengths and in his darkest hour his friends held him up.

Nick also notes the support of a psychologist to navigate the overwhelming feeling of excruciating grief. Nick, naturally competitive, and back then perhaps expecting more of himself than was reasonable, recalls a turning point at the three-year mark of Jodi's passing. Feeling broken despite all his success with the foundation and seeing how resiliently his children were adapting to life without her, nothing could take away the harsh reality that he missed Jodi terribly and their future together was gone forever. Nick asked the psychologist why he wasn't moving through this as capably as he thought he should. It had been three years and the pain stung as deeply then as it did the moment she left. The psychologist gently reminded Nick to give it time. After a loss of this magnitude it usually takes at least seven years to start making sense of a different life from the one they had planned. Nick realised at that moment he had still not made his own grief and self a priority. Nick was pushing himself through the pain in order to be strong for his children and for the foundation. Nick took a breath and started to develop self-compassion. Nick feels this has been hugely influential on his ability to remain stoic and persistent.

Nick also feels his wellbeing strengthened by 'discharging' his stress through rigorous exercise and fundraising, which led to his third survival tool – purpose.

The Jodi Lee Foundation had raised over ten million dollars to date. Nick started something bigger than he first imagined possible and has saved countless lives along the way. It's also been his greatest purpose so far and a place to return to in moments of grief, that with little or no warning still visit him and his children with a pain that will never leave them.

The Jodi Lee Foundation was born from grief, hope, compassion and a lot of hard work. Nick found a way to sustain and nurture himself through the hardest process of his life, losing his wife and the mother to his two young children.

As our conversation came to a close, Nick reflects on how proud he was of Jodi and how resiliently she coped with terminal cancer. It was Jodi who stayed strong when they told their two children Mum wasn't going to make it. It was Jodi who faced the reality first, that her young, unfinished life was almost at an end. It was Jodi who wrote her life story for their children in those final painful months, so they could know her after she'd left – a book Nick still can't bring himself to read. It was Jodi who taught Nick that people can do hard things and that even in the worst of times, there could be love, laughter and adventure.

Despite Nick moving beyond the 'seven-year mark' and moving forward with many aspects of his life, Nick only needs to mention Jodi's name and a raw surge of pain streams across his face. Yet he bravely sits with it, lets it in and then he moves it through with a courage and persistence that's a privilege to experience.

Derrick McManus: former sniper, special operations diver, counter-terrorist operative, STAR (Special Tasks and Rescue group officer, human durability expert, author, keynote and public speaker (www.derrickmcmanus.com)

A high-risk arrest that was 'just another day in the office' for STAR group officer Derrick McManus ended up being a gruelling 41-hour siege, with 2,000 rounds of ammunition shed between police and the offender. Derrick's story is one of physical, mental and emotional preparedness, optimism and determination.

Derrick sustained 14 gunshot wounds from a powerful 7.62 SKK military assault rifle in under five seconds. One bullet completely severed the main (radial) artery in his left forearm. A tiny piece of shrapnel severed the ulna artery in his right wrist. One of those bullets missed Derrick's femoral artery by the width of paper. With the sound of relentless gunfire as a backdrop, Derrick lay bleeding to death, monitoring his organs shutting down and thinking of his wife and children. Massive internal injuries and overwhelming thoughts of death swept over him. It was the steady emotional preparation before this incident that Derrick attributes to his survival.

Derrick had prepared for a scenario like this long before he found himself in it. As his body failed him, he knew it was now up to his mind. There was no space or time for mental clutter. He had to focus on what he needed to do in that moment – survive. Derrick needed to bring his emotions down so any thinking left was rational and constructive.

Derrick calmed his mind with thoughts like, 'I've trained well for this. I know what I need to do. It's still going to be hard, but I know what to do.' Derrick consciously slowed his breathing and heart rate down as he hung on to his life. He had practiced these skills long before this day. He had invested in his emotional resilience long before he needed to use it.

Police, paramedics and doctors arrived at the scene, putting their own lives at risk, determined to pull Derrick away from a siege that was still only in its infancy. When they reached him, Derrick had no sign of life, wasn't breathing, had no measurable blood pressure and hardly any blood left in his body.

Miraculously, he survived, beginning a long haul of recovery which included learning how to walk again, one step at a time. A long and arduous physical rehabilitation process was ahead of him. Jumping out of helicopters, abseiling down mountains to rescue people, and bursting into houses to rescue hostages was also at the back of his mind – but Derrick remained focused on the present and what was in front of him at the time, allowing himself time to recover fully and completely.

Despite the overwhelming desire to return to the frontline, Derrick's family was his first priority. They recharged his emotional batteries that had been sapped by survival and recovery. He took the opportunity to embrace time at home with them and to rest and recover together.

In the back of his mind, Derrick knew that to fully reset and recover he needed to return to the work he loved. If he couldn't do that, he had to find a new and better future. Derrick carefully considered the impact a decision like this had on the people who loved him. He wanted to be responsible with his choices and the consequences of his choices. With his wife's support and encouragement, and his rigorous physical and psychological assessment and intensive rehabilitation, Derrick did indeed return to the STAR group. He went back to his old job with the friends he loved and the role he treasured, knowing full well he might find himself in the same boat the very next day.

What Derrick now knows for certain is that no matter how hard it gets, knowing why you're doing what you're doing will remind you what to hold on to when you want to give up. 'Chase the passion, focus on small goals, celebrate the wins, cry if you need to, feel it all.'

Derrick's time with a psychiatrist specialising in trauma was another turning point – even though he only needed to see him once. Three hours together allowed Derrick to ask about other survivors and what made the difference between those who handled it well and those who didn't. Derrick, curious, logical and sensible, wanted to be prepared in case it happened again. This conversation was also the start of gathering data for his role in the work he does now.

Derrick attributes his reset, recharge and recovery to many things; firstly, being prepared not only mentally and physically, but emotionally. Derrick's emotional intelligence prepared him to be calm during a crisis. Mindfulness, breathing and presence tools helped him focus on what he needed to do at the time – to survive. Connecting with his friends and family was crucial throughout the process. Derrick's ability to see the funny side of things and laugh about the accident in his own way was crucial. His ability to know what he wants, set goals and be willing to trudge through the small steps to reach the bigger ones kept him going on the tougher days. His determination to rebuild a body that was given the stamp of 'broken' defied what everyone predicted for him.

Derrick is a global hero and inspirational leader for post-traumatic growth. In the most powerful and succinct way, he teaches about the power of the mind and necessity to be prepared for challenges before they happen.

When you talk to Derrick, his warmth, authenticity, humour, intelligence and genuine desire to impart knowledge mean you want to stay talking for hours. When you talk to Derrick you never quite feel like you're done. His story is one everyone should hear.

Melissa Little: early childhood Educator, author (www.yesterdayyouwerehere.com)

In January 2016 Melissa Little's world fell apart, incomprehensibly. Her sons, Koda, four, and Hunter, nine months, were victims of murder under the most tragic of circumstances. Melissa's story is one of love, honour, determination and courage.

Melissa begged the universe to wake her up from a nightmare she had unwillingly taken centre stage in. Forced into a world that nothing could prepare her for, Melissa's stoic navigation of every mother's worst nightmare inspired compassion, courage and hope.

Melissa explains grief and what got her through like the sea. 'Sometimes it's calm, but then gets rough. The waves come crashing in. My friends and family did not watch from the shore, they were in the waves with me, helping me stay afloat, while each wave crashed over me.'

An immeasurably broken heart ached for the chance at life that had been taken from her sons. The milestones they would never see. The conversations they would never have. The cuddles they would never hold. The laughter they would never share. Melissa was determined to honour Koda and Hunter's memory in every way possible.

Melissa's strong desire to stay connected to her boys meant she started writing goals that were significant and purposeful and somehow involved them. The first goal she conquered was the hardest by far. Assigned already as Koda's kindergarten teacher, Melissa was offered the opportunity to take leave or teach another year level. Melissa made the brave decision to take the first term off and return to teach his class in his honour. This brought him close to her, allowing her to see what he would have been doing that year. Melissa describes it as 'the hardest year of my teaching career.'

Melissa's next meaningful and purposeful goal was to walk the Kokoda Trail. Koda was named after the trail where his great-grandfather had fought in 1942. Melissa was going to walk it with Koda to celebrate his 18th birthday. Melissa passionately made the decision to walk the Kokoda Trail in his honour.

Preparing for Kokoda meant training and exercise, an unexpected gift to her mental health, wellbeing and recovery. Melissa shares how it gave her a 'clear and focused mind, stronger determination and physical challenges which helped keep a positive attitude and outlook. It gave a purpose to keep going, to get up each morning. I think I found walking the trail itself easier than I anticipated, but this was partly due to the fact that nothing was going to be as hard as what I had just endured.'

On returning, Melissa missed having the purpose, direction and connection she had while preparing for and walking Kokoda. Melissa also felt disconnected from her boys when she didn't have a goal that included them.

Writing *Yesterday You Were Here* was her next unexpected gift in resetting as she worked through her grief. Some days she would see Koda's preschool friends on their outings. Their looks of confusion and heartfelt questions turned Melissa's attention to 'What about the kids? Koda's friends – how are they going? Who helps them? How do they make sense of such a tragedy, when their friend was here one day and gone the next?'

Melissa, determined to help them, put pen to paper and decided to support them through the grieving process with storytelling; something Melissa, an early childhood Educator, knew exactly how to do. Writing a book to honour her sons meant she wanted to do both the writing and illustrations. While she knew how to do the writing part, she didn't know how to draw yet. It was time to take art lessons, another unexpected wellbeing gift. Each lesson brought on nerves and waves of grief, with Melissa fighting the urge to cancel every single lesson. Melissa bravely brought her sons front and centre in her mind, sat with the emotions and got back on track. She discovered that painting was incredibly therapeutic for her and allowed her to practice emotional resilience and release her pain in a way that was somehow uniquely joyful.

Yesterday You Were Here is a heartfelt storybook for children on grief, love, connection and hope. It has reached thousands of children already, helping them process the incomprehensible. Melissa has honoured Koda and Hunter's memory far and wide, above and beyond what she ever knew possible.

Melissa is grateful for her life, new husband, and Koda and Hunter's little sisters born recently. She allows herself time to be present in each stage of grief, a time to be sad and a space for tears to flow when they need to. Melissa thanks her parents for raising her to be courageous, kind and hopeful; to see every day as a new opportunity and to know that while pain is part of life, you allow it, honour it and keep going in the most meaningful way you can find.

While every day hurts in its own way, milestones including the anniversary of Koda and Hunter's death, their birthdays, Mother's Day, Christmas and years of 'firsts' cut to her core. Their memory is honoured and her grief supported through special rituals including releasing balloons, floating wreaths, writing poems, letters and memories to them, releasing butterflies and doves, growing a rose garden and forget-me-not flowers.

Ultimately, Melissa tells me it's nature that brings her a unique comfort. Melissa craves sunrises, finding hope in each new day. Rainbows, the sun peeking through the clouds, bring Koda and Hunter to mind, imagining them watching down over her. Melissa is an exemplary mother, representing fierce, lifelong love and limitless determination.

7 Where to from here?

If you're thirsty for more, here are some websites dedicated to Educator Wellbeing.

https://beyou.edu.au/
https://brenebrown.com
https://growinggreatschoolsworldwide.com/
www.sueroffey.com/
www.smilingmind.com.au/mindfulness-workplace
www.viacharacter.org/
https://schools.au.reachout.com/articles/tips-for-teacher-wellbeing
https://resilienteducator.com/collections/wellbeing/
https://thehighlyeffectiveteacher.com/category/teacher-wellbeing/
www.teacher-wellbeing.com.au/
https://schools.au.reachout.com/articles/mental-health-support-tips-for-teachers
www.mhfa.org.au/#

If you would like to look further into improving mental, physical and emotional wellbeing in your students, there are many practical and evidence-based programmes available, including the 2nd edition of *The Resilience and Wellbeing Toolbox: Building character and competence through life's ups and downs*, (2020) Madhavi Nawana Parker, Routledge, London, and *The Confident Minds Curriculum: Creating a culture of personal growth and social awareness* (2019) Madhavi Nawana Parker, Routledge, London.

The following websites also support young people's wellbeing:

https://studentwellbeinghub.edu.au/educators/resources/
https://beyou.edu.au/resources/tools-and-guides/wellbeing-tools-for-students
www.education.gov.au/aus-student-wellbeing-framework
https://schools.au.reachout.com/wellbeing-5s
www.twinkl.com.au/resources/ks2-pshe/health-and-wellbeing-pshce-subjects-key-stage-2/health-and-wellbeing-pshe-subjects-key-stage-2

https://waamh.org.au/mental-health-promotion/school-wellbeing/resources
www.blackdoginstitute.org.au/education-services/
https://positivemindsaustralia.com.au/free-resources/
www.monash.edu/health/mental-health/resources

Wishing you well, always,
Madhavi Nawana Parker

Index

4-7-8 breathing method 54
2020 Global Pandemic, educator wellbeing and 1, 4–13; adjusting to new routines, demands of 7; emotional rollercoaster of 6; Forde, Skye, experience with 10–11; Hutchinson, Shawn, experience with 8–10; impact of, beyond classroom 6; McKenzie, Emma, experience with 13; middle school teacher experience with 13; overview of 4; Porter, Jo, experience with 12; post traumatic amnesia and 7–8; Radford, Lucy, experience with 11; school psychologist experience with 12; school support officer experience with 11, 12–13; shared personal feelings concerning 8–13; war comparison to 4–5; what ifs 5–6

achievements, celebrate 16–17
activities for fun 55–56
alienation theory 80–81; from nature 80; from others 80; from ourselves 81; from work 80
anxiety, experiencing 21–22
asymptomatic 6
attention, mindfulness and 52
Australian Unity Wellbeing Index 55
autonomy 5

behaviours that push your buttons, identify and prepare for 22–23
'big breaks' 29
body's reactions 29
breathing 49–50; conscious 51; diaphragmatic 50; meditation 51; mindful 54; rate, as focal point 28

career reset questions 15–16
challenges as form of coaching 68–69
change, adapting to 70–71

channel in your mind, changing 44–45
chill songs 54
circuit breakers, feelings and 28
clear your mind 36–37
comfort zone 71
communication 25
compassion 25–26, 46–47
connection, empathy and mutual respect values 30
conscious breathing 51
control 5; letting go of 41
Covid-19 4, 6, 7, 8
creativity 57
crisis and challenge stories 86–93; Hicks, Gill 86–88; Lee, Nicholas 88–90; Little, Melissa 92–93; McManus, Derrick 90–92; overview of 86
cultivating thoughts 20

daily routines, changes to 26
decision making process 69–70
decluttered/organised environment, wellbeing and 80
diaphragmatic breathing 49, 50
difficulty, healthy response methods to 18–19
digital detox 44
discomfort/struggle, getting comfortable with 17–18
drinking, mindful 53–54
Dweck, Carol 32–33

eating, mindful 53–54
educators: emotional rollercoasters of 6; frustration during pandemic 6; revisit your purpose as 67; student wellbeing and 2
educator wellbeing: 2020 Global Pandemic and 4–13; comebacks 65–84; during

crisis and challenge, stories of 86–93; future for 94–95; healthy, resetting for 14–34; introduction to 1–3; recharge thinking tools, rituals and practices 35–47; resting/recovering and 49–63; websites dedicated to 94; *see also* wellbeing; *individual headings*
email or text messages, replying to 77
emails of thanks 40
emotional intelligence 24–25
emotional rollercoasters 6
emotions, reacting to 29–30
empathy 30; wellbeing comebacks and 82
expectations of yourself/others, adjusting 21

feelings: acceptance 24; awareness 24; moving through difficult 19; other people's, attention to 25; uncomfortable 24
fight or flight response 28
flatten the curve 4–5
flow, resting/recovering and 61
focal points 28
Forde, Skye 10–11
forgiveness 23
Fredrickson, Barbara 23–24
functional relationship 68

Global Pandemic impact stories 8–13; from Forde, Skye 10–11; from Hutchinson, Shawn 8–13; from McKenzie, Emma 13; from middle school teacher, New South Wales 13; from Porter, Jo 12; from Radford, Lucy 11; from school psychologist, Melbourne, Australia 12; from school support officer, South Australia 12–13; from Shari, school support officer 11
Global Pandemic, learned lessons from 66–67
goal scans/audit for wellbeing comebacks 74–75
goals, wellbeing comebacks and 73–74
gratitude 38
growth mindset 32–34; thinking skills 33–34

'have to' for 'get to,' exchanging 39–40
health, responsibility for 79
healthy wellbeing going forward *see* wellbeing comebacks
heartbeat, as focal point 28
help, asking for 76

Hicks, Gill 86–88
hopeful outlook for day 37–38
humour, maintaining 41
Hutchinson, Shawn 8–10

inactivity time 56

Jodi Lee Foundation 88–90
journaling: for fun 56; gratitude questions 38; learned lessons from Global Pandemic 66–67; mindset questions 45

kindness as core value 77–78
know myself 75

Lee, Nicholas 88–90
legacy, finding/leaving your 78
Little, Melissa 92–93
loving kindness meditation 57–60; overview of 57–58; receiving loving kindness 58; sending, to all living beings 59–60; sending, to loved ones 58–59; sending, to neutral people 59

Marx, Karl 80
massage, resting/recovering and 63
Matthews, Gail 73
McKenzie, Emma 13
McManus, Derrick 90–92
meditation 57; breathing 51; loving kindness 57–60; *see also* loving kindness meditation
mental health, self-compassion/self-care and 2
mentoring 43–44
mind, decluttering 36–37
mindful breathing 54
mindful eating/drinking 53–54
mindfulness: attention, giving full 52; benefits 52; described 51; presence and 51–52; techniques 27
mindful walking 27, 53
mindset, recharge at end of day 45
Montreal Neurological Institute 54
movement: for resting/recovering 60; wellbeing comebacks and 82
music for resting/recovering 54–55, 62
mutual respect 30

nature focus 40, 56
negative news watching 55

obstacles, racing ahead/looking back moments and 26–27

optimism: cultivating 27; practicing 37–38; wellbeing comebacks and 83

pause for presence breaks 53
peer support/mentoring 43–44
people's opinions, reliance on 31–32
perspective, keeping things in 41–42
plimsoll line 37
podcasts for resting/recovering 62
poise 81
Porter, Jo 12
positive emotions 23–24
positive words jar 39
possibilities questions 15
possibility mindset, strengths-based 14–15
post traumatic amnesia 7–8
presence, mindfulness and 51–52
pride 62
progressive muscle relaxation 50
pulse, as focal point 28
pyjama/comfort wear days 62

Radford, Lucy 11
radio for resting/recovering 62
reactions, space and 81
reading for resting/recovering 60
recharge thinking tools, rituals and practices 35–47; change the channel in your mind 44–45; compassion and 46–47; control and 41; digital detox 44; emails of thanks 40; exchanging 'have to' for 'get to' 39–40; gratitude and 38; hopeful outlook for day 37–38; humour, maintaining 41; mind, decluttering 36–37; mindset end of day recharge 45; nature focus 40; overview of 35; peer support/mentoring 43–44; perspective and 41–42; plimsoll line, finding 37; positive words jar 39; rest and 47; self-talk 35–36; smiling 42; supportive conversations 43
recovering see resting/recovering
rehearsing 20
reset questions 16
resilience 41–42
resistance 20
rest 47, 56–57
resting/recovering 49–63; 4-7-8 breathing method 54; activities for fun 55–56; breathing 49–50; breathing meditation 51; creativity and 57; flow and 61; full attention to moments 52; inactivity time and 56; loving kindness meditation 57–60; massage and 63; meditation 57; mindful eating/drinking 53–54; mindfulness, presence and 51–52; mindful walking 53; movement for 60; music for 54–55, 62; nature and 56; negative news and 55; overview of 49; pause for presence breaks 53; podcasts for 62; pride and 62; pyjama/comfort wear days 62; radio for 62; reading for 60; rest and 56–57; shake off and 61–62; sleeping, conscious breathing and 51; water and 60–61
risk taking, healthy/calculated 69
routines, changes to daily 26

sanguine, wellbeing comebacks and 83–84
self-care 30–31; prioritising 1–2
self-compassion 46–47
self-talk, recharging 35–36
shake off 61–62
sleeping, conscious breathing and 51
smiling 42
social connections 83
social isolation 8
social media, wellbeing comebacks and 76–77
strengths-based possibility mindset 14–15
strengths, finding and using 75–76
stress management 5, 28
struggle, getting comfortable with 17–18
student progress 31–32
student wellbeing: educators and 2; websites supporting 94–95
supportive conversations 43

text messages, replying to 77
thank you emails 40
thinking habits 27
thoughts/feelings, accepting without judgement 26
'to do' lists 32

upsets, avoid cultivating, resisting and rehearsing 19–21

vulnerability 76

walking, mindful 27, 53
water, resting/recovering and 60–61
wellbeing: control/autonomy and 5; definition of 2; described 1–2; music consumption to improve 55; prioritising 1–2; questions for sustainable change 3; self-compassion/self-care and 2; shake off 61–62; young people's, websites supporting 94–95; see also educator wellbeing

wellbeing comebacks 65–84; alienation and 80–81; caring for self over students 72; challenges as form of coaching and 68–69; change and 70–71; comfort zone and 71; decision making process and 69–70; decluttered/organised environment 80; email or text messages, replying to 77; empathy and 82; goals and 73–74; goal scans/audit for 74–75; health and 79; healthy/calculated risk taking 69; help, asking for 76; kindness as core value 77–78; know myself step 75; learned lessons from Global Pandemic 66–67; legacy and 78; lifelong learning and 79; look back at career 71; look forward/savour small events 73; movement and 82; optimism and 83; overview of 65–66; poise and 81; reactions, space and 81; revisit your purpose in education 67; sanguine and 83–84; social connections in friendly company 83; social media and 76–77; strengths, finding and using 75–76; vulnerability and 76; what matters to you, working out 72–73
wellbeing mindset, cultivating 27
wellbeing, resetting for healthy 14–34; anxiety, experiencing 21–22; behaviours that push your buttons and 22–23; 'big breaks' and 29; body's reactions and 29; circuit breakers, feelings and 28; compassion and 25–26; connection, empathy and mutual respect 30; daily routines, changes to 26; difficulty, healthy response methods to 18–19; discomfort/struggle, getting comfortable with 17–18; emotional intelligence and 24–25; emotions, reacting to 29–30; expectations of yourself/others, adjusting 21; focal points and 28; forgiveness and 23; growth mindset and 32–34; obstacles, racing ahead/looking back moments and 26–27; overview of 14; people's opinions, reliance on 31–32; positive emotions and 23–24; possibility mindset, strengths-based 14–15; reset questions 15–16; self-care and 30–31; stress and 28; student progress and 31–32; thinking habits and 27; thoughts/feelings, accepting without judgement 26; 'to do' lists and 32; upsets, avoid cultivating, resisting and rehearsing 19–21; 'what could go right?' 19; wins/achievements, celebrate 16–17
wins/achievements, celebrate 16–17

Yesterday You Were Here (Little) 93

For Product Safety Concerns and Information please contact our EU
representative GPSR@taylorandfrancis.com
Taylor & Francis Verlag GmbH, Kaufingerstraße 24, 80331 München, Germany

www.ingramcontent.com/pod-product-compliance
Lightning Source LLC
Chambersburg PA
CBHW051756230426
43670CB00012B/2319